Frenchy's Grease Scrapbook

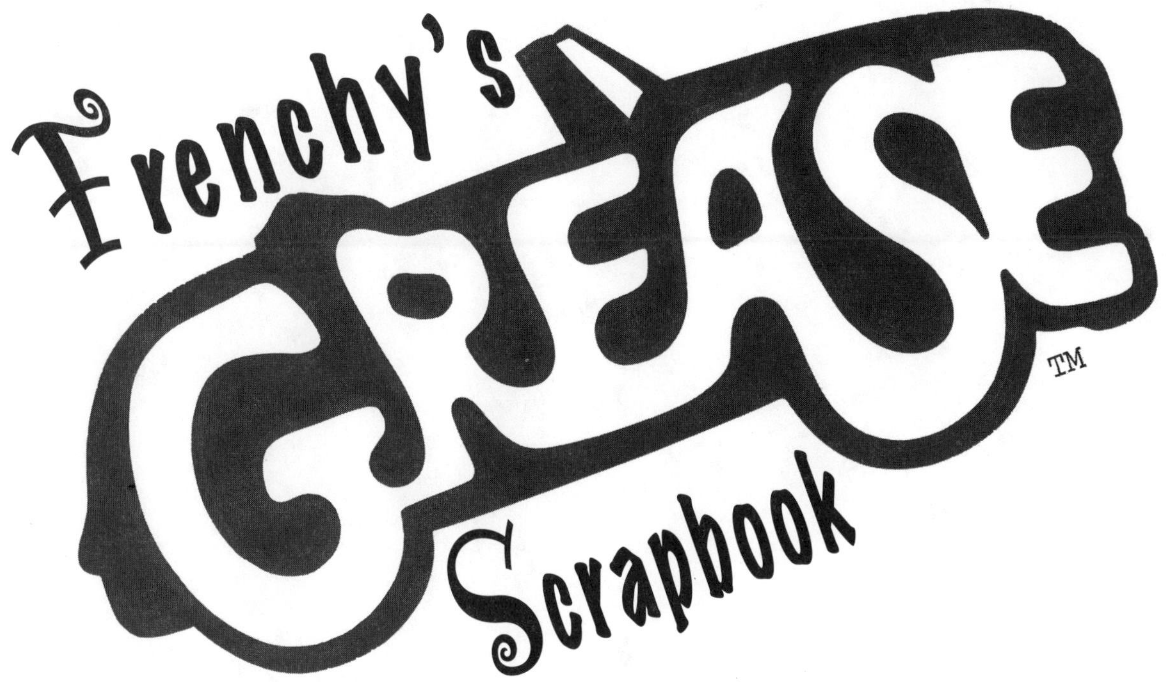

"We'll Always Be Together!"

Didi Conn

New York

 For information address Hyperion, 114 Fifth Avenue, New York, New York 10011.

Library of Congress Cataloging-In-Publication Data
Conn, Didi.
Frenchy's Grease scrapbook : we'll always be together / by Didi Conn.—1st ed.
p. cm.
ISBN 0-7868-8345-6
1. Grease (Motion picture) I. Title.
PN1997.G686C66 1998
791.43—dc21 97-36480
CIP

Book Design by Christine Weathersbee

FIRST EDITION

10 9 8 7 6 5 4 3 2

Page 180 constitutes an extension of this copyright page.

CONTENTS

HOW IT ALL BEGAN

by Allan Carr

Didi Conn and Allan Carr.

Once upon a time, on a warm summer night in 1974, I went to see a Broadway musical called *Grease*.

I took two up-and-coming powers of the musical theater with me, Marvin Hamlisch and Michael Bennett, and the three of us fell in love with the spirit of the show. We felt like dancing in the aisles. We went to Joe Allen's afterward and talked some more about how much fun we had and how terrific the audience response was. Right then and there I made up my mind. I said to them, "I have to make this into a movie!"

The next day I called Ken Waissman, one of the of the show's producers, to find out about the disposition of the film rights. Ken said, "Oh, we are so sorry, it's already been optioned by Steve Krantz and Ralph Baakshi." They were planning on making it a screen cartoon. So, that was that.

Two years later, I was in New York again at the opening of Bette Midler's *Clams on the Halfshell* revue at the Minskoff Theater. I'll never forget it. I was on the escalator going down to the lower lobby and realized that right in front of me were Ken Waissman and Maxine Fox, the producers of *Grease*. I tapped them on the shoulder and said, "By the way, what ever happened with the film rights to *Grease*?" "Funny you should ask," Ken said, "the rights lapsed today and Steve and Ralph didn't pick up their option, so the film rights are available again."

The next day I called ICM, the agents for the authors, Jim Jacobs and Warren Casey. I told them I wanted to buy the movie rights to their show. Fortunately for me, the show

Allan and the T-Birds: Michael Tucci, Barry Pearl, and Kelly Ward.

was considered the bastard child of Broadway at that point. It was a long-running hit, but it was the year of *Man of La Mancha* and *Company* and other "serious" musicals. So they said I could have it for sum of $200,000; but in those days, I didn't have that kind of money. So I asked if I could pay it on an installment plan, like I was buying a used car, and surprisingly, and happily for me, they agreed. And even more important, they also agreed that if some of the music from the stage musical wasn't quite right for the movie, we had the right to add additional songs to the picture. Without that interpolation clause, something that composers for the legitimate theater never agree to, "You're the One That I Want," "Grease," "Sandy," and "Hopelessly Devoted" could never have been in the movie.

Robert Stigwood had already helped me by putting up the money for the Spanish-language release of a film that I saw in Mexico City and thought it would make a great exploitation release in the United States. After most every studio had turned *Survive* down, it turned into a major commercial success for Paramount, and as a thank-you to Robert, I asked him if he would like to produce *Grease* with me. So I went back to David Picker, the head of Paramount and the man to whom I had brought *Survive*, and went on and on about my vision for *Grease* until he said, "We'll make this deal!"

Bronte Woodward and I worked on the adaptation and the screenplay. I based my changes on *my* high school in the Chicago suburbs, where the kids were not all greasers, like in the stage musical. They were tough but good kids, and by moving the setting to the suburbs, I made it closer to my own high school memories and, much more important, more resonant for a wider audience. To that end, I also cleaned up some of the raunchy language.

We finished shooting *Grease* in the fall, but *Saturday Night Fever* still had not been released (*Fever* didn't come out until December). No one knew yet that John Travolta's career was going to go through the roof, and Paramount was still nervous, all except for Frank Mancuso, the future director of distribution, who said, "Forget about the nay-sayers. I'm booking this picture into great theaters all over, including the best theater in Westwood."

We ran previews in Honolulu because Paramount wanted them to take place as far from L.A. as possible in case the reaction was poor. They put phony titles on the film cans, but a local disc jockey found out what was really being screened, and, by the night of the preview, there was a line that went around the block twice. So many people were turned away that the film had to be run again later that night and again the following morning. The minute the animated part of the title sequence came on and a little deer came out of Sandy's bedroom we had them from then on. And we didn't change a thing.

Allan Carr, honorary Class President of Rydell, hanging out with the gang!

Who said producers don't get along with their stars?!

We opened against *Jaws II*. I remember Charles Bludhorn, the head of Gulf and Western, saying, "We have to beat the shark, we have to beat the shark!" We did the exact same business the first week. By the end of the whole run our grosses were twice theirs. Paramount had a parade of hits lined up for that summer—Warren Beatty's *Heaven Can Wait* and the first Chevy Chase–Goldie Hawn picture, but *Grease* went on to become the studio's biggest-grossing picture. It grossed about 180 million dollars in film rentals here in the United States and then did equally as well in Europe, which made it a 400-million-dollar picture. And it only cost six million dollars to produce, making it one of the most profitable movies of all time and the biggest-grossing musical in movie history—a title it still holds!

Allan and Olivia.

Like many kids, I was not too popular in high school. But producing *Grease* made me feel like I was the president of my class. And it was the most fun that I have ever had working on any entertainment project, before, during, and since. It was magic, and I remember it like it was yesterday. Now, twenty years later, it's like we're all back together again. Not that, in a sense, we were ever apart—with a video and an album that are perennially on the top of the charts and a film that sometimes seems to be playing on television as often as "60 Minutes." And coming full circle, revivals of the Broadway version have now been running for five years in New York and London.

Michael and Allan at the dance contest waiting for Marty.

That's how *Grease* became a motion picture. It was a movie I had to make, and with the collaboration of a whole host of brilliant and wonderful people, it turned out to be about as perfect a realization of my dream as I could hope for. Now, with it's re-release, *Grease* is a "dream come true"—twice!

INTRODUCTION

Has it really been twenty years since we made the movie *Grease*? It's hard to believe.

In the spring of 1998, a major celebration will take place promoting the re-release in theaters nationwide of this now classic film. For me, it will be a Rydell High School reunion. I can't wait to see everyone! I've stayed in touch with some of the T-Birds and Pink Ladies—Olivia and John in particular—but I can't wait to put on my pedal pushers and Pink Ladies jacket and "shake some cake" with some of the most talented and loving people I have ever met.

Over the years strangers have become so excited when they realize they've seen me in *Grease*. "She's from *Grease*!" some kid will blurt out to her parents. "She's from Greece?," they say. "How do you know that?" "No, Ma, not the country, the *movie*!" Sometimes I don't even have to be seen to turn heads. People tell me there is no mistaking my voice—I guess that's the one thing that hasn't changed in twenty years!

Once my little brother and I encountered a huge line snaking down West 43rd Street where *E.T.* was playing. We were dying to see it and couldn't go to a later showing. I had five movies come out in the previous two years, and I was on a hit television series. So I shamelessly walked up to the ticket booth and asked if the movie was sold out for that performance. The young man selling tickets looked up at me and said, "That voice! I would

Joel Thurm (left), me, and Randal Kleiser.

know you anywhere. Oh my God, come right in. You don't have to wait on line!" He came out of his booth to greet us at the door. I tried to hand him a twenty-dollar bill as we walked in, and he said, "Oh no, you don't have to pay, I *love* your work. Go right in, Miss Tomlin!" Woops!

Perks are the goodies that come from being a recognizable show-business entity, little unexpected treats like upgrades on airlines, a table in an over-crowded restaurant, or a place for your 8 x 10 on your local dry cleaner's Wall of Fame. But I have had many, many more meaningful rewards from my work, and perhaps the richest and most long lasting have been the very special friendships that my *Grease*-mates and I initiated twenty years ago one hot summer in Los Angeles.

It took us three months to make *Grease*. We rehearsed all the scenes and musical numbers for three weeks, and the rest of the time was spent filming. We were all a tad older than the characters we played, so we had a blast pretending to be teenagers again. I have to confess to you right now that we were all very "good" while filming that movie. We might have talked about sex thirteen out of the fourteen hours a day we were together, but for the most part, it was all talk and no action. All the flirting and teasing was stimulating enough by itself, and I think it helped to make our scenes juicier. The shooting of *Grease* was all of our high school experiences heightened and condensed into one really magnificent fun-filled summer.

Me and my mom, Beverly Shmerling.

In the midst of it all, my beautiful mother, who would come and visit me from time to time while we were filming, took some terrific candid photos on the set and at our premiere party. It got me thinking, Wouldn't it be great to put together a scrapbook of *all* of our memories? And so I began collecting photos and interviewing the cast and creative staff, hoping that I could get all of this material published someday.

Well, someday is here! *Frenchy's* Grease *Scrapbook* is my commemorative collection of our Rydell memories and an update on where all my buddies are today. It was so great catching up with everyone while writing this book. Not only did people take their prized photos out of frames on their walls for me, everyone was extraordinarily loving and supportive. Now, looking through these pages, I realize more than ever how much I miss my *Grease* friends, but I also find that this scrapbook brings them a little closer. I'm so happy to share these wonderful memories with you, and I hope this book helps you feel closer to me and my friends, too. For whenever I leaf through these pages, I know that "we'll always be together!"

Didi Conn

Here we are posing for our cast publicity photo for Paramount photographer Dave Friedman.

Here we are posing for Pat Birch's son Jonathan Becker. (No offense, Jonathan!)

GREASE

Screenplay by

Bronte Woodard

Screen Story by

Bronte Woodard and Allan Carr

Adapted from the Broadway musical by

Jim Jacobs and Warren Casey

A ROBERT STIGWOOD/ALLAN CARR PRODUCTION

Return to Script Department
PARAMOUNT PICTURES CORPORATION
5451 Marathon Street
Hollywood, California 90038

THIRD DRAFT

May 12, 1977

THE HISTORY OF *GREASE*, THE STAGE MUSICAL

Interviews with Jim Jacobs, one of the two original creators of *Grease*, Maxine Fox and Kenneth Waissman, the Broadway show's original producers, Tom Moore, the Broadway show's director, Pat Birch, the show and film's choreographer, and Louis St. Louis, the show and film's musical director

Jim Jacobs, one of the two creators of *Grease*, spoke to me about his close friendship with his partner Warren Casey and how their collaboration on the show began. He really misses Warren, who died a number of years ago, and he's still working on plays they started writing together. I don't think he was completely kidding when he said that he occasionally contacts a Ouija board to see if Warren agrees with certain line changes he's making.

Warren and Jim met while doing community theater in Chicago in 1963. Warren had just moved to Chicago and was going to broadcasting school. He had wanted to be a disc jockey, and Jim was working as an advertising copy writer at the *Chicago Tribune*.

Jim Jacobs (above) and Warren Casey (left).

They met in an amateur theater and, as Jim put it, "immediately—it was, like, bizarre—we hit it off."

Warren and Jim were best friends for seven years before the idea for *Grease* ever came up. As Jim tells it, "It was in 1970, I was hosting a wild cast party in my apartment late one night, and Warren was there. I had gone into my closet and dragged out all my old dusty disks, as we used to call them, my old 45 records from the 1950s—Little Richard, Dion and the Belmonts, The Flamingos—and I started playing them in the midst of all the acid rock and psychedelic. Everyone at the party was going, 'What's this stuff?' and I said, 'Doo-wop. Don't you just love doo-wop?'

"Later I said to Warren, 'Wouldn't it be a gas if there was a Broadway show that used these kinds of tunes instead of the traditional *Oklahoma* stuff?'

"Warren said, 'Yeah, you know, that's a really funny idea, but what would the show be about?'

"I said, 'Well, it would be about the kids I grew up with and hung around with. We could call it *Grease* because in those days everything was greasy—the hair, the food, the cars, you know, everything.'

"At the time, Warren was working for a chain of women's undergarment stores but soon got fired from that job, and he said to me, 'I've always envied you. It must be great to just sit at a typewriter and think of clever things and come up with funny phrases. That's what I want to do. I'm going to go and buy a typewriter because I have to practice my typing.'

"So he went and bought a typewriter and about a week later he said to me, 'I was practicing my typing so I wrote a scene for that show we were talking about.'

"And I said, 'What show?' Because I had completely forgotten about it.

"'*Grease*,' he replied.

"I said, 'You mean, we're going to do this?' No one was more shocked than me, and that night he let me read the first scene he wrote, the girls' pajama party scene. Of course it was ten times longer than it wound up being. It was almost a one-act play. The whole scene was there—piercing the ears, smoking, drinking, all the girls hanging out together, even 'Freddy, My Love' was almost there (in the play, the song is sung by Marty at the pajama party). That was the beginning, and I said, 'Holy cow, now it begins in earnest, we're really going to do this!'"

"The musical *Grease* began in Chicago in a community theater," says Jim, "and the famous myth that our producers Ken and Maxine like to tell is that it was five hours long. In actual fact, it was probably two hours long, but because everyone had to sit on the floor or benches it *seemed* five hours long. *Grease* opened in Chicago at the Kingston Mines Theater on February 5, 1971. It was originally scheduled to run for only four performances in Chicago—two weekends. Of course, the word spread, and there was almost an immediate demand for tickets."

Maxine Fox and Kenneth Waissman were the producers of the Broadway musical. Maxine told me, "When we saw the show in Chicago we got very excited. Ken's image of it was a really good one. He said, 'It's like you opened a big trunk and every memory you had about the fifties popped out.' We wanted to bring it to New York, so we developed a plan. Jim and Warren had to agree to move to New York to do the rewrites. We had to find them a very special director who could work with them on the book. It would be an off-Broadway production, and they had to take the risk of moving to New York and getting it done—we couldn't pay for it. To their credit, they understood what we needed, knew that they wouldn't have to do it alone, that we'd be giving them a director to work with them, and they agreed to do it.

"Our quest for a director began. As luck would have it, that same week we went to The American Place Theater and saw an incredible play about a quadriplegic called *Welcome to Andromeda* by Ron Whyte. It was riveting from beginning to end. The next day we called the producer of the play and asked who directed the piece because we had to meet him. She gave us a number where Tom Moore could be reached in California, and we subsequently met Tom and fell in love with him."

The first Frenchy, Marya Small, with Tom Moore at the Broadway opening.

Tom had just graduated from college and tried to turn the show down. "I didn't think it was something I should do coming out of Yale," he told me. "I wasn't sure I understood it. Ken and Maxine wanted me for my knowledge of the fifties, but I knew nothing about the greasers of that period."

That didn't deter Maxine and Ken. They were so impressed with Tom's directorial abilities that they wanted him regardless. Maxine said, "It would have been easier if he knew more about the fifties than he did, and he certainly wasn't the type to drink beer or use four-letter words."

Tom remembered the first time he heard the music. "I was in Ken and Maxine's apartment and I loved it. It was just ultimately too appealing. I wanted to direct it. Casting *Grease* was a challenging process. I was looking for young people who were eminently likable. Actors that could dance rather than the other way around. For example, we had a big cattle call in the lounge of the Eden Theater to cast the show. We heard a voice coming from the top of the stairs that was so unique, we knew it was our Frenchy. Marya Small had the part when she walked in the room."

Maxine, Ken, and Pat all agreed that Tom's invaluable contribution was his extraordinary ability to develop three-dimensional characters that made you really care for all the sixteen people in the play. Maxine adds, "In order to make them unpredictable, the actors had to bring something of themselves to each role and collaborate with Tom to make those characters larger than life. But it had to be anchored in some reality. Something about these characters sets them apart. The writers relived their memories superbly, but it was the collaboration with the *Grease* energy that came from Tom, Jim, Warren, and Pat Birch that made this show take off."

Pat Birch choreographed both the Broadway musical and the movie version of *Grease*. I asked her why she wanted to work on the musical. "It was a story that could work in any period. If you look at any high school class, you find the outsiders getting left out, people vying for position. That's what we really dug into. It was not just being cute and fifties. It was getting underneath what teenage lives are really like, especially in the late fifties, when there were no wars or AIDS. In the fifties, the biggest problems were if you could get the car for the night, or could you afford to buy a new record. But those kids magnified them. You look in any high school and you find your Frenchys and your Rizzos and Zukos—they're all there.

"I felt *Grease* was much more than a musical about the fifties. I think it's about high school and the passionate emotional connections you make there. The song 'We Go Together' was the perfect anthem for these friends who needed each other so badly and wanted to always stay together. I choreographed that number with the kids piling up all over each other. They need to feel each other and hold on to each other."

Pat Birch was hired as the show's choreographer.

One of the last key creative staff members to join the *Grease* team was Louis St. Louis. He was the last musical director to be interviewed for the job. As Louis remembers it, "Jim and Warren just didn't like anybody. You know, when I say they didn't like anybody, I mean it seemed that no one could click with them. It was late October of 1971, and I had just come back from being a soloist in the premiere production of Leonard Bernstein's *Mass*, which he composed for the inauguration of the Kennedy Center. I was brought in to meet Jim, Warren, Tom, and Pat. I was sitting on a sofa in Maxine and Ken's office listening to a tape of the music. By the time 'Freddy, My Love' came on, I had slid down to the floor with Jim, Warren, and Pat. Pat and I looked at each other and we did an imitation of George Saunders and Bette Davis—ya know, 'I got your number, my dear. This will do just fine!' Warren and Jim agreed and I was signed on."

Tom Moore, Pat Birch, Maxine Fox Lorence, and Kenneth Waissman.

Maxine Fox Lorence told me their were eight national touring companies besides the Broadway company. "For every company of *Grease* several thousand actors were seen to get the sixteen that were needed. Everyone cast had to act, sing and move well, and possess that special radiance that makes the show work." This resulted in the casting of some very talented young actors, many of whom became nationally known later in their careers. Here's a rundown of some of them, part by part:

DANNY
Barry Bostwick
Jeff Conaway
Treat Williams
Patrick Swayze
Peter Gallagher
Rex Smith
Richard Gere

SANDY
Ilene Graff

PATTY
Ilene Kristin

KENICKIE
Jerry Zaks
Danny Jacobson

ROGER
Walter Bobbie

SONNY
David Paymer

MARTY
Marilu Henner

DOODY
John Travolta

TEEN ANGEL
Alan Paul (Mantrano)

RIZZO
Adrienne Barbeau
Judy Kaye

JAN
Mimi Kennedy

The Chicago leg of the First National Company tour—1973-1974. That's Carol Culver leaning with her elbow on the car; and next to her, Marilu Henner, Barry Pearl (Doody in the movie), Greg Evigan, Candi Earley as Sandy, and Judith Sullivan as Cha Cha.

(Left) John, as Doody, in the First National Company tour of *Grease*, 1973-1974. (Above) To the right of John, Barry Bostwick (*Spin City*) as Danny and Barry Pearl as Sonny.

Grease opened off-Broadway at the Eden Theater in New York on February 14, 1972. Maxine Fox told me that the budget for the entire production was around $100,000! Jim Jacobs's dream to have fifties music on Broadway finally came true when the musical opened on Broadway at the Broadhurst Theater that following June and ran for 3,388 performances. *Grease* became the longest-running musical in Broadway history on December 8, 1979.

Within six months of the Broadway opening, a national tour crossed the United States and Canada, with seventeen-year-old John Travolta playing Doody. Child employment laws required the producers to hire John's sister Ellen to be his chaperone. Ken Waissman remembers, "John showed up one day at the auditions for our first national touring company. His only experience had been summer stock in New Jersey, his home state. But our director, Tom Moore, recognized his unique qualities and superior acting talent."

A year later, the first London production opened with a young unknown, Richard Gere, as Danny Zuko.

Jim told me a little-known fact: "*Grease* is probably the only hit Broadway musical ever composed entirely on guitar. It never occurred to us when we were picking out those tunes on our guitars that *Grease* was going to be the ideal show for schools to put on. It's hard to see it ever going out of fashion, because the early days of rock 'n' roll seem to appeal to everyone, regardless of age."

Think about all the good ideas that may have exploded in your mind and then zipped away as fast as they appeared. Jim, however, had a great idea and was fortunate enough to have Warren, who saw what Jim was after, as his best friend. Warren wrote the first scene, the collaboration caught fire, and not only did Jim's dream to see *Grease* on Broadway come true, but its characters, story, music, and lyrics have become an indelible part of international pop culture. So many people connected with the original play or the movie owe the flowering of their careers to Jim and Warren. And it's a little mind-boggling to think how many *Grease* devotees owe them their gratitude for the countless hours they have been entertained by what these two men wrote.

AUDITIONS

When an actor gets a call from their agent telling them they have an audition for a major motion picture, the actor has two reactions simultaneously:

1. "Oh great! I have an audition!"

   and

2. "Oh s—, I have an audition!"

The "Oh great!" response comes from the fact that your agent doesn't call you every day with such good news. Normally, he or she submits your picture and resumé to a casting agent assigned to that project. Casting agents begin the process of elimination by reviewing the hundreds of submissions received. Then they call the agents of the actors they want to see. (There have been "creative" actors who have "crashed" auditions, but unless the producer and director are totally desperate and you are absolutely, positively the exact person they are looking for, you will get thrown out and humiliated and barred from ever coming to that office again.)

The 8 x 10 photo I used for my audition for *Grease*.

PARAMOUNT! I think everyone associates Hollywood with that beautiful and famous studio. Not only is it the studio that produced the film *Grease*, but I made my television debut on a series that was filmed there. It has nothing to do with how I eventually got the part of Frenchy for the film, but the story of how I got my first job with Paramount is actually pretty funny, so let me tell you what happened:

Back in New York in the early 1970s, I made over fifty TV commercials my first year in the business! I would go to three or four auditions a day where I would play someone's girlfriend, child, or wife. You meet lots of people you might have to kiss and hug one minute and say good-bye to the next. One day, as I was riding down on an elevator from an audition, I began chatting with a handsome guy I was sure I knew from commercial work. I said to him, "It's so good to see you again, what's new?"

He politely responded by saying, "You're very sweet, but we have never met. I'm Henry. What is your name?"

I said, "I'm Didi! I know we have worked together. I know you!"

He said, "I am sure we have never met."

I said, "I am sure we have!"

He said, "Who cares? Would you like to have a cup of coffee?"

(continued on next page)

The "Oh s—!" response spontaneously erupts from all your past disappointments. Unlike a job interview where your experience, personality, and expertise in your given field are the main reasons you are hired or not, actors are too often judged primarily by their appearance, their age, and their "look." Many directors, producers, and casting agents will agree that they can usually tell in the first ten seconds after an actor enters a room whether they are right for the part or not. An actor who has just spent the last twenty-four hours studying and preparing a scene may be judged before he even opens his mouth!

In other words, talent can be the second most important thing to the audition process. Then there are the factors other than talent that can make or break an audition—for instance, what if an actor's appointment is scheduled right before lunch and the director is cranky and hungry? Or, what if you remind them of an old girlfriend or worse, their ex-spouse! It's a tough business, and luck and timing and "who you know" really do make a difference.

Here's what led up to my audition for *Grease*. I moved to Los Angeles in the summer of 1974. Getting work was slow at first, so I applied for unemployment insurance. One week, while I was waiting in a cramped, burnt orange office to collect my check, a very good-looking guy with a sexy dimple in his chin and a goofy smile came in and sat down next to me. Guess who it was? John Travolta! He had just moved to L.A., too! It wasn't long after that that he landed his first series, *Welcome Back Kotter*, and I got my first series with Danny Thomas, *The Practice*.

I worked a lot for the next three years. One day I got a call from my agent, Bob Gersh, who told me Paramount Studios was making a movie called *Grease* and I had an appointment to meet the director, producer, choreographer, and casting agent at Paramount the next day. Bob told me I would be reading for the part of Frenchy, the beauty school dropout. I had to go to the audition dressed in 1950s clothing and do my best to look the part. He said I could pick up the scene I would have to learn for my audition at the main gate of Paramount Studio. ("Oh great! Oh s—!")

Me and Danny Thomas at MGM studios where we made *The Practice.*

I stood at the gates of Paramount and read my audition scene for *Grease* right there. But it was very short and didn't give me much information. The guard told me I had to go—I was holding up traffic. As I was leaving, I noticed a smaller pile of envelopes on his little desk. I asked the guard if those big fat envelopes happened to contain the whole script to *Grease*. "Yes," he said. "Oh please, can I see the whole script?" I begged. I didn't really know who my character was from the little information I had. I didn't know what happens right before the scene I had to learn or what happens right after. I had to say a speech to Sandy, "Men are rats, worse than that, they're fleas on rats . . ." Why is she saying that and who is Sandy? Why are the other Pink Ladies making fun of her? And why are men rats? I pleaded with the guard, "If I could borrow the script for a little while to search for some clues to who this Frenchy character is, I would be so grateful."

He couldn't let me take someone else's script away, so I asked if I could hide under his desk, where no one would see me, and read one. He

So we did. We had fun telling each other jokes, and then I asked him what he was up to lately. He said, "Well, I've been very busy doing *Happy Days* . . . " Oh boy, he was right! I never met him—I had only seen him on television playing The Fonz! Should I tell him or just keep pretending? I was too embarrassed, I didn't say a word. "So, tell me about Hollywood," I said. "What's it like? I'm thinking about moving there myself this summer." Well, Henry Winkler, The Fonz, gave me his phone number and told me to call him if I did come to L.A.

Guess what? Three months later I was living on Larrabee Avenue in West Hollywood, California. My first audition for a guest part on a television series was, as luck would have it, for *Happy Days*, being filmed at Paramount Studios. I called Henry and told him when my audition was to take place, and he was in the producer's office when I got there. He asked the director if he could read with me. Boy, was I nervous, but when he started to play around with me, I relaxed a little and had fun. I left the office thinking I didn't get the job because I was too nervous, but thanks to Henry, I did! I got my first job on a television series as Joyce, Ralph Malph's girlfriend.

(Above) Me and Ron Howard. (Right) Me and Donny Most on the set of *Happy Days*, filmed at Paramount.

looked at me as if I were from outer space because in the twenty-five years he had been there, no one had ever asked him anything like that. But he must have felt sorry for me because he said that I could. So there I was, in that guard's gate house the size of a toll booth, squished under his desk frantically racing through that script.

But, boy, was it worth it. I learned a lot, especially that Rizzo was a bigger and better part. So as I prepared to look and act like Frenchy, I was also secretly fantasizing about playing Rizzo.

Since I didn't have any fifties-style clothes in my wardrobe, I went to Western Costumes in Hollywood. I picked out black pedal pushers, a pink blouse, and a matching pink sweater with some rhinestones on it and also a pink chiffon scarf to go around my neck. My real problem was my hair. Every day is a "bad hair" day for me. I have very straight, limp, unruly hair, and I knew Frenchy would take pride in having a terrific 'do. I decided not to get a red wig (just in case they would consider me for Rizzo) and instead go to a professional hairdresser. The next part of my story may be hard to believe, but it's true. I got up very early the next day and went over my lines, got dressed in my fifties clothes, and left my house to find a beauty parlor. I drove down a street I had never been on before, and there right in front of me was a purple building and a big pink neon sign on it that said, FRENCHY'S HOUSE OF BEAUTY! I couldn't believe my eyes!

There was an attractive woman with an elaborate hairdo vigorously applying the last bit of spray to a "work of art." "Excuse me," I asked, "are *you* Frenchy?" "I sure am!" she chimed. "How can I help you?" I decided not to tell her about the audition and instead used the time to get to know her. I asked her a million questions. What made her get into the beauty business? Which beauty school did she go to? She told me everything. She always loved hair. She used to cut the hair on all her dolls before she started on her two younger brothers. She said the snapshots in her family photo albums were so funny because everyone's hair looks lopsided and terrible. But with practice she became an "artist." She considered herself a beautician, a mother confessor, and a chemistry whiz. She loved to bring out the best in people. I told her I wanted my hair to look just like hers—big! She must have used a whole can of hair spray on me, but it worked. I looked hot!

I'll never forget the first time I saw Allan Carr, Pat Birch, Randal Kleiser, and Joel Thurm. (They were the producer, choreographer, director, and head of casting.) I must have looked good in their eyes, because as soon as I walked in they started laughing. Believe me, there is nothing better than to walk into an audition and feel like you might be what the people in charge are looking for. Things were going so well that I figured if they like me now, wait till they see me as Rizzo! They let me read a Rizzo scene but they asked me if I could come back the next day to dance for them as Frenchy. When my agent called me later to give me the appointment for my callback, he told me I had made a great impression—they really liked me. Also, they already had someone else in mind for the role of Rizzo. I wasn't disappointed. I was enjoying becoming Frenchy.

• • •

As I drove past the guard gate into Paramount the next day, I threw a big kiss to my co-conspirator and said, "Thanks to you, they want to see me again!" He told me to knock 'em dead! And I said, "Don't worry, I'm going to nab this sucker!"

There were about five hundred people crammed onto a sound stage learning the "hand jive." The room was alive with fifties music and nervous energy. Everyone looked like they knew what they were doing—except me. I asked a darling young blond guy if he would go outside with me and slowly show me the steps. He turned out to be none other than Kelly Ward, the actor that was to play Putzie. I learned how to do them, except every time we were supposed to change direction, I would go in the opposite direction by mistake. As hard as I tried to get it right, I just couldn't do it. I began to think, I'm standing out like a sore thumb, I'll never get this job unless I can do it right. Well, I guess they didn't want everyone to be doing it perfectly, because when we shot the big dance contest scene in the movie, Pat Birch asked Doody and me to do it the same way I did it at the audition—the opposite way!

We had a singing callback after that. Then came the most gruesome part of this whole audition procedure: the process of elimination. We were called in to the studio in groups of four—four potential Pink Ladies, then four hopeful T-Birds. If you went in and they liked you, you were asked to stay. If they didn't, you were told something to the effect of, "Thank you very much, we'll let you know, you can go home now."

I felt embarrassed for the well-known actors I saw leaving. I wished they had told us all to go home and then called us back at another time to save everyone the humiliation of public rejection.

After about five hours, they had narrowed it down to four Frenchys, four Martys, and four Jans. And four of each for the men's roles. Then they began to mix and match potential Pink Ladies with the potential T-Birds. They asked us all to sing "Happy Birthday" and then to improvise some scenes together. It was so unreal, but I was having so much fun improvising that I didn't have time to be nervous.

The next day I was at a gas station in Santa Monica and something told me to call my answering service. Sure enough there was a message to call my agent. I called him and was told the good news. They wanted me to play Frenchy!!

• • •

I've always wondered how everyone else got cast in the movie. Amazingly, when we were filming, none of us ever talked about how we landed our roles—or who our competition was. But it was fascinating now to talk to everyone and learn how they all got one of the most memorable jobs in their careers.

John Travolta/Danny Zuko

Producer Robert Stigwood said, "John Travolta's performance in *Saturday Night Fever* boasted just the right mixture of animal magnetism and innocence." Before that, John had been America's number one heartthrob as Vinnie Barbarino. No question that he was the perfect choice to play Danny Zuko on the screen.

But he was not the original choice to play the part. Allan Carr told me a very interesting story about who it was offered to before John Travolta:

John in the mid '70s.

"At the time, Henry Winkler, The Fonz, was Paramount's biggest star, and they would have been thrilled to have him star in *Grease*. I was on the lot and personally handed the script to him. 'What's this?' he asked, and I told him that it was the adaptation of the Broadway musical *Grease*. He told me how flattered he was to be asked to star in a movie I was producing, but he felt he was playing the same kind of character every day on television and maybe it would be better to play a different kind of role."

How do you like that?! Henry is a terrific actor and he would have been great as Danny. But you must be wondering how John Travolta became Danny Zuko. Here's the story Allan told me:

John's agency photos for commercials.

Henry Winkler (with Ron Howard), the original choice for Danny.

"Several years before I optioned *Grease*, a young press agent in New York, Bonnie Chasen, had told me about a young actor who could also sing and dance and whom she thought was terrific. I wasn't casting anything at the time, but she had given me his picture which I stuck in a drawer in my bedroom. I was getting hundreds of pictures at the time, since my primary work was managing stars like Ann-Margret, Mama Cass, Peter Sellers, and Rosalind Russell, among others. And then, several years later, I opened that drawer and there was that picture of John Travolta, who by now was starring in *Welcome Back Kotter* on television. His television movie of the week, *Boy in the Plastic Bubble*, had been a major success, and I had learned he had even played the part of Doody in *Grease* in the first national company and always wanted to play Danny Zuko.

"I met John for the first time through Eddie Bondi, his agent at William Morris, who took me to a recording studio where John was making an album and out to dinner with them afterward. I thought John was a perfect choice to star in the movie. I told Robert Stigwood that I had found a terrific actor for *Grease*, and he put together a three-picture deal for John at Paramount, *Saturday Night Fever* being one of the pictures."

John told me he was thrilled to be offered the part. "I had so much experience with the play. I was very familiar with all sorts of interpretations for that role. I saw maybe five or six different guys play Zuko on the stage and saw what worked and what didn't. I swore I would do it differently and added my own feelings to it. I kind of used what I thought worked well, threw out what I didn't like, and created something new."

When stars are being considered for a movie, they often request to meet their co-star before they agree to do it. Olivia Newton-John wanted to meet John for the first time privately at her home in Malibu. Here's how Olivia describes the first time she saw John:

> "I remember it very well. I first met John when he came to my house at Big Rock. He walked up my little driveway and I thought, Oh he's cute. He's sweet. He's so sweet!"

I told John how Olivia felt at their first meeting and here's what he said:

> "Really? She said that? You know, I thought she was so conservative I would have never imagined that she was feeling any of that. I went out to Malibu to meet her, and I was very impressed with her because she was already very much a big pop star. And she was so adorable everybody had a crush on her, including me. But I didn't know what she thought of me, and she was kind of reluctant to do the movie, and, you know, I was just glad to meet her and hoped we would work together on this project."

John Travolta as Danny. (Isn't he gorgeous?!)

Olivia Newton-John/Sandy

Can you believe it? John never knew how attracted Olivia was to him! They were perfect as Danny and Sandy. I really can't imagine anyone else in those roles. But Allan did have someone else in mind to play Sandy before he offered the role to Olivia:

"Ironically, with *Saturday Night Fever* still in the future, Paramount didn't consider John a star and was anxious to have a star for the role of Sandy. I thought Susan Dey would be wonderful, but her agent, who was also her husband, turned down the project for her on the grounds that she was now an adult leading lady and didn't play high school girls anymore. Fortunately, Susan Dey, who is a lovely person, went on to have a great career and lots of success, especially on *L.A. Law*. We looked and looked but there was nobody who had a "name" and had that right kind of innocence. I thought Deborah Raffin had those qualities, but Paramount wanted a bigger name. I said, I don't know anyone else, I've been through everybody! Since we had all looked and looked and hadn't come up with anyone else, I figured if I kept persisting, Deborah would get the part.

"And then one night Helen Reddy and her husband, Jeff Wald, invited me to dinner, and I found myself sitting across the table from Olivia Newton-John. Although I certainly had heard about her from her records, I knew very little about her except that she was very good in concert and in night clubs. But throughout dinner, I kept staring at her, I couldn't take my eyes off her. She was so sweet and warm—she was Sandy.

Olivia in 1977.

"At the end of dinner I told her that I was producing a movie and would like her to be the lead. She was shocked but agreed to read the script, and, by the time it was delivered to her, we had changed it so that Sandy was now Australian. Olivia was interested in the part, but since she had done a picture in England that she felt she was not very good in, she insisted that she be given a screen test and the right to say no to the picture if she didn't like herself in the test. That was unheard of, but Paramount agreed, and I didn't care because I knew she'd be terrific. So she and John did the famous ring-giving/ring-flinging scene at the drive-in movie. It was so perfect that we could have used the screen test in the finished film!"

Olivia Newton-John as Sandy. ("Too pure to be pink!")

Olivia told me about that first movie she made, which was called *Tomorrow*. "It was really terrible, and I wanted to make sure that if I did another movie, it wouldn't be terrible. I asked Allan if I could do a screen test—even if he didn't want one, I wanted one! I had fun with John filming the test. We made each other laugh. He really was wonderful. I thought we worked well together, and I was excited about the transformation Sandy was going to make at the end of the movie. So, I enthusiastically accepted Allan's offer to play Sandy."

I loved working with Olivia. She is so sincere and so beautiful. She was the perfect Sandy.

A Polaroid from Olivia's requested screen test.

Stockard Channing/Rizzo

So, now the two leading characters were cast. Allan felt he had the ideal actress to play Rizzo:

"I had picked Lucie Arnaz to play Rizzo, she was perfect. Paramount wanted her to test with John and Olivia just to see how the three of them looked together, but her mother, Lucille Ball, wouldn't let her do a test, saying something like, "I used to own that studio, my daughter doesn't have to test." Paramount put their foot down and said, "No test, no part!" But Lucie wouldn't do the screen test. We were almost ready to start shooting, and we were stuck because I had never looked at anyone else.

"And then I happened to speak to Stockard Channing, and I remembered I had seen her in a play, *Vanities*, in which she, Sandy Duncan, and Lucie had all played teenage girls living together in a dormitory. Stockard came in to audition, did her number, knocked us out, and that was it. She was Rizzo. That was Friday, and she had to start shooting the following Monday!"

Stockard Channing as Rizzo.

Stockard was right in the middle of filming a Neil Simon movie called *The Cheap Detective* when Allan asked her to come in to meet Randal Kleiser and Pat Birch. The movie was a take-off on *Casablanca*. She was playing a naive secretary to Peter Falk's Bogart. As Stockard described it:

"My character had rolled-up dark hair with a little flip on the bottom of the wig, I was innocent and wide-eyed, and I wore a plain shirtwaist dress. It was Friday and rehearsals for *Grease* were going to begin on Monday! I was called in at the last moment because Allan remembered the second movie I was in, *Sweet Revenge*. The movie was never released, but Allan saw it at Cannes, where it received a lot of attention. I played a juvenile delinquent car thief. Obviously, 'the nickel dropped in his head' because he realized I could play a character like Rizzo. Allan got ahold of *Sweet Revenge* and screened it for Randal and Pat, and after that I got the job!

"I spent the whole weekend listening to the *Grease* album over and over. On Monday morning I was Rizzo—very tough, damaged goods, a person who never felt sorry for herself. When I finished rehearsing Rizzo's tough-girl scenes at Paramount, I would drive across town to be the dumb secretary in *The Cheap Detective*."

Over the years, I have seen Stockard play a wide range of roles. She never ceases to amaze me. She is a great actress, powerful, versatile, and funny.

Jeff Conaway/Kenickie

Everyone makes mistakes in life; decisions that if we were given the chance to reconsider, we would make differently. Luckily, Jeff Conaway was spared the heartache of making a wrong choice by his manager. He came very close to turning down the opportunity to play Kenickie. Here's what he told me happened:

"Bob LeMond, my manager, called me up and said, 'I made an appointment for you to meet the producer and director of the movie *Grease*.' I said, 'For what? John's already playing the role of Danny.' Bob said, 'They want to see you for Kenickie.' I said, 'Kenickie?! I'm not Kenickie! Kenickie's a no-neck monster.' So I told him I don't think so, I just don't see it. I said, 'No, I'm not going to meet them for that role. Cancel the meeting!'

"After I hung up I thought about it for twenty minutes. I thought, Hold on here, I got a chance to be in a movie

Jeff Conaway, circa 1959, 2nd from left. "This is what *I* was doing in the fifties," says Jeff.

of a hit Broadway show—who cares if it's Kenickie? I don't have to play it the way it was played on the stage, I can do it differently. So I called Bob back up and said, 'Look, I changed my mind.' He said, 'Conaway, I know you *so well*—I never broke the appointment.'"

I was curious why Jeff wouldn't want to play Kenickie. I knew that he played the role of Danny on Broadway, but Kenickie is a sexy and demanding leading role.

"You see, the way Kenickie was always played was kind of a short, squatty, square kind of guy who was more of a sidekick. Kind of scrappy, kind of like a bulldog with one eye hangin' out. And obviously, you know, I gotta work with what God gave me. So I figure, okay, we just change him. We make Kenickie and Danny best friends. Zuko is the leader because of his special brand of charisma, but Kenickie is *really* the leader. Because when it really comes down to it, he'll kick everybody's ass. So that's the way I made it work for me. I made him more of a leading man instead of playing a second fiddle kind of role."

Now the leaders of the T-Birds and the Pink Ladies were set.

(Top) Jeff as Danny (with Ilene Graff) in the Royale Theater's production of *Grease*. Jeff as Kenickie (right).

Dinah Manoff as Marty.

Dinah Manoff/Marty

Joel Thurm began casting all the other roles in the movie. As I mentioned before, a casting agent weeds through all the submissions before he sets up meetings. Joel told me if he doesn't know an actor, he will set up a preliminary meeting where he can first meet the actor alone. He called in Dinah Manoff to read for the part of Frenchy, but when she walked into his office and he saw how voluptuous and sexy she was, he changed his mind and asked her to read for Marty.

Dinah remembers Joel giving her some helpful clues as to how to play Marty:

> "He asked me what kind of lipstick I was wearing. I told him it was called Fire and Ice. It was my great Aunt Freemo's old lipstick from the fifties. He told me about an old Revlon commercial for Fire and Ice lipstick. I wasn't sure what he was talking about but listening to him made me feel like I had hot lips! I began to feel like a movie star. I started to think, That's who Marty would want to emulate: movie stars of the fifties—Jayne Mansfield, Brigitte Bardot, and especially Marilyn Monroe. I thought, Yes, that's who Marty wanted to be—Marilyn Monroe."

Joel was very impressed with Dinah. He felt she embodied a feeling of "confused sexuality. Her hormones were pumping and she didn't know where it was coming from or what to do about it! Which was just the right feeling for Marty."

Dinah was shocked when she was called back to meet Randal and Allan. "When my agent called to tell me they wanted to see me again, I was stunned! I remember thinking, Why would they call me? I can't believe they are calling me back for this, because I was just fooling around at my meeting with Joel. I really didn't know what I was doing. I was just playing with his suggestions and ideas for Marty. But I had no idea he liked me."

After Dinah did her Marilyn Monroe impression for Randal and Allan, she was called back again to dance and sing for Pat Birch.

> "That dance audition, oh, I remember that dance audition. When I heard about a dance audition, I went, 'Oh, f—!' First of all, I can't dance. And second of all, I can't really sing. There must have been at least five hundred people there. I kept thinking, They're not going to give me this part. After several hours, it was narrowed down to me and Debralee Scott. I thought, Oh my God. Debralee Scott, at the time, was a big star on *Mary Hartman, Mary Hartman*, and I knew I was going to lose the part to her. But, much to my surprise, I didn't; they wanted me to play Marty!"

When Dinah was telling me this story I couldn't help thinking about her at the dance contest, sidling up to Vince Fontaine, and the innocent way she told him her name, "Maraschino, like the cherry." Her lips were undulating like two juicy ripe cherries ready to be picked. If Rizzo was the toughest Pink Lady and Jan the funniest and Frenchy the most career-oriented, then Marty was definitely the sexiest!

Michael Tucci/Sonny

While we're on the subject of Marty, the sex goddess, her on-screen boyfriend Sonny, played hilariously by Michael Tucci, had a totally different experience landing his part.

Just as casting was beginning, Michael was about to open at the Westwood Playhouse in Los Angeles in a Jules Pfeiffer play called *Hold Me*. Joel Thurm was a fan of Michael's after seeing him in a musical called *Minnie's Boys*. So Joel took Allan Carr to see the opening night of *Hold Me*. When it was over, Joel went backstage and told Michael that Allan loved his performance and wanted to meet him at Paramount the next day. As Michael tells it:

> "So the very next day, my parents drove me to Paramount. I got there early and read the script. The screenplay was very different from the stage play. I played a character named Roger in the play, and as I'm flipping through the pages, I don't see Roger's name anywhere in the screenplay. I go into Allan's office and I tell him I just read the script and there's no guy in there that's a wise guy, eats a lot, and mimics everybody. I told him all the guys seem the same. Allan said, 'What do you mean? How would you make him different, what would you say?' So I improvised, 'Hey Rizzo, I hear you're knocked up, what's goin' on, hey, how 'bout we go for a slice of pizza.' They all laughed a lot and Allan stood up and said, 'You're Sonny, you're Sonny! Roger and Sonny from the original play will now be one character and we'll call him Sonny.' He shook my hand and I walked out of the office. My mother and father were outside in the car. When I told them I got the job, we all went crazy!"

Michael Tucci in the mid '70s.

Barry Pearl/Doody

Doody—what a name for a boyfriend! "Mom, Dad, this is . . . Doody, my boyfriend." Did you ever wonder what his real name was? Doody's real name was Anthony Delfuego, but the nickname Doody is short for Howdy Doody, which is how the producers first envisioned the character: a redheaded, freckled kid who looked just like the puppet.

Barry Pearl, who played my main squeeze in *Grease,* was a complete and utter doll. He was a great dancer, and nobody came close to contributing more original ideas, lines, and funny business than he did. He was very familiar with the original play because he played Sonny in the first national company—alongside none other than John Travolta who was playing Doody!

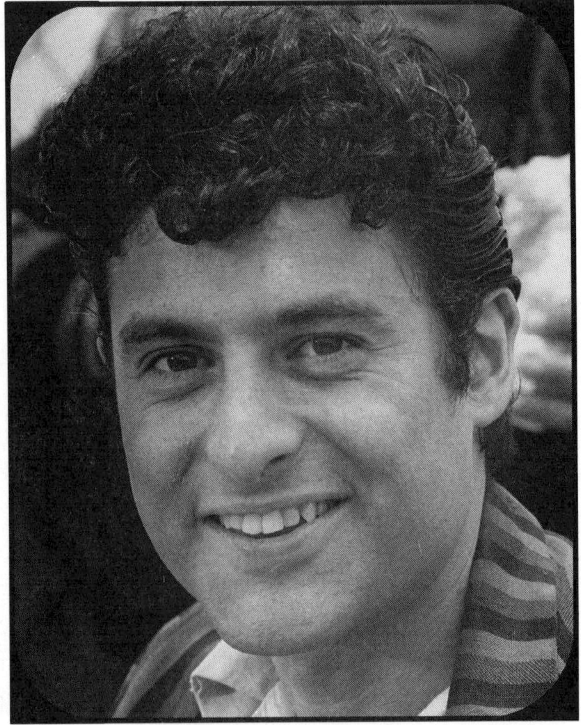

Barry Pearl as Doody.

But Barry's agent told him that Allan Carr was not going to use anybody who had been in the stage version of *Grease*:

> "We were told that no one in the play was going to be involved in the movie, but my agent submitted me anyway. First I met Joel Thurm and then I came in to see Jim Jacobs, Pat Birch, and Allan Carr. I had my hair slicked straight back, the way I wore it in the play. They were interested in me for the role of Doody. The third time I was called back I was asked to dance and sing, and it was now down to about thirty guys and thirty girls.
>
> "Pat put all the girls on one side of the room and all the boys on the other. One at a time, each guy and girl had to come out to the center of the floor. Then the guys had to convince the girls to dance a little bit and then convince them to go off with us. I started to think about what I could do that might be different. In the Broadway musical, at the end of the dance at the gym, the original Sonny, Jim Borelli, got drunk, and at the end of that scene, as all the people leave, Sonny walks up the stairs and encounters Cha Cha, who in the play had this huge yellow dress on and was as big as a school bus. She was an unattractive girl, not the hot, gorgeous character that Annette Cardona created in the movie. So Sonny in his drunken stupor encounters her and then falls backward down the stairs.
>
> "And I'm thinking to myself, At this audition what I would like to have happen is for me to be the last guy up and to have the last girl be a *meiskeit* (Yiddish for ugly). As luck would have it, it was down to me and another guy and there were two girls on the other side. One was very pretty and the other wasn't pretty at all.

I'm praying I get matched up with the not so attractive girl and I can pretend I'm drunk and be totally enamored with her.

"Well, that's what happened, and I stagger out like I'm drunk with a Styrofoam cup in my hand. When I reach her, I put the cup in the cuff of my jeans and it stays there. That got a good laugh. Then I take her in my arms and start to dance. I place my hand firmly on her tush. She removes my hand and places it on *my* tush. In my drunken stupor, I think I got *her* tush, and I start caressing my own tush as if it were hers. Well, they went nuts.

"We had one more callback after that. I remember Tucci, Kelly, Jeff, and myself were all there. John was there, too. Everybody was dismissed except for the five of us. They had us go over to the piano in the corner of the room and sing. (Musical director) Louis St. Louis was playing, and we all had fun. When we were finished, Allan said, 'Well, that sounds great because that is the sound we're going to have in the movie.' So that's how I found out I was cast as Doody for the film. Right then and there. I really couldn't believe it. The whole time I did the national tour of *Grease*, I hoped I would be asked to be in the Broadway production, but I was never hired to do it. I always felt very bad about that. So, to this day, I wish I could have been a fly on the wall at the Royale Theater when the kids that were doing the play on Broadway found out that Barry Pearl's going to be in the movie and on top of it, cast not as Sonny, but as Doody, to boot! Oh, yeah!"

Kelly in his teen hunk days, the mid 70s.

Kelly Ward/Putzie

Kelly Ward definitely had luck on his side when he called Pat Birch to ask her if she needed any help at her dance auditions for *Grease*:

"Do you know how I managed to wrangle a reading for myself? I had been out of work for a while, and then I got a job on a Broadway show called *Truckload*. The director was Patricia Birch, and that is where I met her. It was Pat's directorial debut. It was produced and mounted by basically the entire entity that did *Grease*, other than the producers and director Tom Moore. Later on, when auditions were announced for *Grease*, I called Pat. I heard that she was going to choreograph the film, and I said, 'I could use a gig, can I come down and help you audition people?'

"And that is really all I expected to land out of it. So I helped with the dance auditions, along with Carol Culver. We worked with Pat on dance combinations. I knew John from working with him in *The Boy in the Plastic Bubble,* directed by Randal Kleiser. So Randal knew me, John knew me, and Pat knew me. So it was just a matter of trying to get Allan to come over and sign on, because I think I had fans in Pat and Randal. That must have been true, because Allan asked me to read, and the next thing I know I am cast as Putzie! It was a real thrill for me, the first film I ever did."

I'll never forget how patient Kelly was with me at that dreaded dance audition. He taught me step by step, clap by clap, how to do the "hand jive"! Pat Birch thought he made the perfect Putzie. She described Kelly as being just the right mixture of "naive and horny."

Kelly Ward as Putzie (above).
Jamie Donnelly as Jan (below).

Jamie Donnelly/Jan

The silliest and sweetest Pink Lady was definitely Jan. A few years after we filmed *Grease*, I saw Jamie Donnelly in New York performing in a one-woman show where she played around thirty-two different characters. She was awesome! She is so smart and so nimble—I think she can do anything! She, on the other hand, didn't think she would ever get cast in the movie.

"I had been Jan one time before in my life. I played Jan on Broadway five years before we made the movie, and I was replaced and my contract was not renewed, so I was convinced no one liked me as Jan. Bob LeMond, my manager, said, 'Jamie, they're going to do the movie,' and I said, 'Well, that's nice for whoever's doing it, but that wouldn't be me.' And he said, 'Jamie, I think you ought to give it a shot,' and I said, 'No, Bob, it's like opening up an old wound. I really am not very good as Jan, I don't know that

I could be Jan again.' And he said, 'Jamie, go on in, John's going to be in it.' And you know, I knew John for a very long time because of Bob, who was John's manager as well. So he said, 'Oh come on, Jamie, John's going in and Jeffrey's going in, just go in and meet on it.'

"I was about thirty years old at that time, and I had felt like I was too old to play Jan. But one thing I knew was who Jan was—I really did. I knew the show so well. I mean, when you play something eight times a week, you really know the feeling of it and you know the spirit of it, and you know where the heart of the material is, and you know what's fun about it. I knew it! So, I went in, and they said, 'What do you want to read for?' and I said, 'Anything but Jan.' And they said okay, and I read for every other role but Jan, but they said, 'We're interested in you for Jan.' I still thought there's no way that this can work out, because I'm just not going to get this part. Anyway, finally by the end—you remember, the day we were all matched—I couldn't believe I was still there. But I decided to just have a good time. When they told me the part was mine, I thought, Boy, Jan is more a part of me than I realized. I guess I had already done the work, and Allan, Randal, and Pat could see it very clearly. So now all I had to look forward to was having fun!"

Annette Cardona/Cha Cha

After Dennis C. Stewart was cast as Leo, the leader of the Scorpions, Joel Thurm brought Annette (Charles) Cardona in for the part of Cha Cha Di Gregorio. Joel told me, "In the original play Cha Cha was played by a large young woman in a yellow dress. One of the great things Bronte and Allan changed in the script was to turn Cha Cha into a beautiful vixen. She had this incredible quality. She was hot and gorgeous, and she was the only one I called in to meet John."

Annette Cardona was using the stage name Annette Charles at the time of her audition. Her audition was different from everyone else's. Here's how she described it to me:

"My audition for *Grease* was not the norm. There was no script. There were no songs. There was nothing. I came dressed in tights and I tried to look 'good.' I was brought onto a

Annette Cardona as Cha Cha.

set, on one of the big sound stages, and so was John. They put very wild, up, disco-ey music on through loudspeakers and blew it through the whole sound stage. Then they asked John and me to dance until they asked us to stop. We had to improvise the whole scenario. Both of us gravitated to each other like honey. I guess they were trying to see the chemistry between us. They were trying to see how compatible we were, how we looked together, how we reacted to each other, and it was instant. No matter what John did, what he threw at me, I was there to give it right back. No matter what ball I threw at him, he threw it right back to me. So we had this give and take. I just remember the whole staff was watching us. We all had a great time.

"As a matter of fact, we had such a wild time that John ran into me and banged me in my head. He knocked me out a little bit, and I remember him putting me on the floor and looking over me and waving his arms. I didn't know what the hell he was doing, except I was pretty knocked out. I was really kind of dizzy for a moment, and I remember we were really great sports and they loved all that. I think they thought we did it on purpose!"

Susan Buckner/Patty Simcox

Now that all the "greasers" were cast, it was time to find the "goody-goodies," as we liked to call them. Susan Buckner was a flawless Patty Simcox, a perfect combination of brown-noser and all-American beauty queen. Here's how she remembers her audition:

"I had danced professionally for years, so a dance audition was a comfortable place for me. It was a great workout. I worked up quite a sweat. When I was called back, I read for several different parts. I didn't hear any feedback about my audition for a few days, and I never liked the waiting game, so I went to visit my dad on his boat in Acapulco. I stayed until my agent called. Yippee!

"I got the part of Patty Simcox, but if Olivia did not get the part of Sandy, I was in the running for that role. I even rehearsed both parts for a while. I knew the character of Patty Simcox. She was exactly like a girl I went to high school with who ran for everything and made the rest of us sick. Except Patty was even more nauseating."

Susan Buckner, 1977 (left) . . . and as Patty Simcox (above).

Lorenzo Lamas/Tom

Remember when I told you there are many ways you can get cast in a movie? Well, Lorenzo Lamas had a most enthusiastic spokesperson singing his praises to Allan Carr:

"My mom, Arlene Dahl, was a good friend of Allan Carr, and she introduced me to Allan at the Academy Awards in the spring of 1977, just before *Grease* went into production. She said, 'Allan, meet the star of your next movie!' I hadn't been in any movies. I was still drooling, I was so young. Allan looked at me and said, 'Do you lift weights?' I told him, 'Actually I'm an instructor at Jack LaLane!' He called me two weeks later and said President Ford's son Steve dropped out of the role of Tom Chisum, and he would like to bring me in to talk about that part.

"I went in the next day to meet Allan, Randal, and Bronte. I asked if there was something I could read for them. They said, 'There's no lines!' I said, 'What?' They said, 'There are no lines. You just kind of hang around. Also, we have to dye your brown hair blond because you look too much like John.' They took me to a fancy hair salon in Beverly Hills. There I was, nineteen years old, 210 pounds of muscle, sitting under a hair dryer with foil on my head! I thought, 'Holy cow, is this what I really want to do for a living?' But as soon as we started rehearsing and I saw what a great opportunity this was for me, I really got behind it. I loved every second of making our movie."

Lorenzo's first "on camera" with dad Fernando in 20th Century Fox's *100 Rifles*, 1968, costarring Jim Brown, Burt Reynolds, and Raquel Welch (left). Lorenzo Lamas as Tom (right).

Eddie Deezen/Eugene

Eddie Deezen, who brilliantly played the part of Eugene, had seen the play at the Pantages Theater in Hollywood. So when he got called in for his meeting he was prepared.

"I knew what the style was, so I slicked my hair back with all this greasy kid stuff and it was really gooped down, and I went in for an audition. It was like a big cattle call. I went into a room and talked to Allan Carr and Randal Kleiser. I read a little bit, and they laughed and we got along real good and that was pretty much it. Then, afterward, my agent called and said they loved me! I had the part!

"The next day they called my agent back and said they were sorry, but they were going to write out the part of Eugene. Later that night, my agent, Regina Penner, and I went to The Mother of Good Council church in Hollywood and lit candles, literally, my agent and I! We prayed for something good to happen and to please have them write the character of Eugene back in the movie. The next day they wrote Eugene back in and I got it . . . again!"

"Hey Eugene!" Eddie Deezen as Eugene.

Allan Carr finished casting the principal roles with some of America's most beloved and talented actors.

Edd Byrnes/Vince Fontaine

Edd was in a very successful television series, *77 Sunset Strip*. He created the character of Kookie, becoming what many consider to be the first of television's youth cult heroes. He received more than 15,000 letters a week, more fan mail than any Warner Brothers star in the studio's history. The private eye series ran for five years.

Eve Arden/Principal McGee

Eve Arden won an Emmy award as everyone's favorite English teacher in her hit television series *Our Miss Brooks*. She starred in numerous films as diversified as *Stage Door*, *Cover Girl*, *Night and Day*, and *Mildred Pierce*, for which she received an Academy Award nomination.

Sid Caesar/Coach Calhoun

Sid Caesar's Emmy-winning *Your Show of Shows* series is a television classic. His many film credits include starring roles in *It's a Mad, Mad, Mad, Mad World* and Mel Brooks's *Silent Movie*. During the making of *Grease*, he was filming Neil Simon's *The Cheap Detective* along with Stockard Channing.

Joan Blondell/Vi

Joan Blondell was a veteran of films, theater, and television. In the fifties she was nominated for an Academy Award for *The Blue Veil*. She starred in *Desk Set* (opposite Spencer Tracy and Katharine Hepburn), *The Cincinnati Kid*, and the John Cassavetes film *Opening Night*, to name just a few of her many credits.

Dody Goodman/Blanche

Dody Goodman first achieved stardom on Jack Paar's original *Tonight Show*. She starred in *Mary Hartman, Mary Hartman* as the "always perplexed" mother. She was also featured in *Silent Movie*.

Frankie Avalon/Teen Angel

Allan Carr thought Frankie Avalon would make the perfect Teen Angel, and was he ever right! I had a mad crush on him. He was the definitive teen idol in the fifties and was a national heartthrob. Frankie was named "King of Song" by the Disc Jockeys' Association and received *Photoplay* magazine's Gold Award for Most Popular Vocalist. His film credits include the famous series of "Beach Party" movies opposite Annette Funicello, and starring roles in *The Alamo* and *Voyage to the Bottom of the Sea*.

Alice Ghostley/Mrs. Murdock

Alice Ghostley was discovered on Broadway in *New Faces of '52*. She went on to star off-Broadway in *The House of Blue Leaves* and won a Tony for her performance in *The Sign on Sidney Brustein's Window*. On television, Alice starred on *Bewitched*. Her film credits include *To Kill a Mockingbird*, *The Graduate*, *Gator*, and *Rabbit Test*.

Sha Na Na/Johnny Casino and the Gamblers

Allan chose Sha Na Na to appear in the movie because the group had become internationally famous for their vocal and visual interpretations of rock music from the fifties. They had sold over nine million albums worldwide and had such hits as "Get a Job," and "Rock and Roll Is Here to Stay." Sha Na Na was one of the featured groups in the legendary film *Woodstock*, performing their hit single, "At the Hop."

Allan also picked many of his television favorites to play other parts—Fannie Flagg, Darrell Zwerling, Ellen Travolta, Dick Patterson, who were all great.

The Dancers

Pat Birch, who received a Tony nomination for her musical staging of the original Broadway production of *Grease*, told me about the unique method she came up with to translate her stage choreography to film:

> "Even though the essential thrust of the musical numbers are somewhat the same as they were in the show, you have to use a whole different process to keep the vitality the same. We decided to have twenty dancers for the film and to use them throughout the movie. They became subcharacters in a sense. When you see them dancing, you should already know them. You've seen them in the classrooms as well as at the hop. All the dancers must create a non-speaking character for themselves. They must pick a name, create a history. When it was time to cast the dancers, we agreed that Rydell would have to have its cheerleaders and its jocks as well as its tougher types."

If you are not a member of the Screen Actors Guild, the American Federation of Television and Radio Artists, or Actors Equity, you have one opportunity to be seen. It is called an "open call" audition, because the audition is open to the public. You can find out when they are being held in a weekly theatrical publication called *Backstage*. Pat Birch held open calls for *Grease* in New York and Los Angeles. Needless to say, thousands of nonprofessional actors waited in line for hours for a chance to be discovered.

Carol Culver, Daniel Levans, Cindy DeVore, Judy Susman, Richard Weisman, and Lou Spadaccini (in front).

Pat was very clear about what she was looking for at both open calls. "We not only wanted good dancers but swell characters—kids who looked like they belonged at Rydell High. *Grease* is a look at high school life. In the open call announcement in *Backstage*, we asked everyone to come dressed in fifties-style clothing. But in actuality, the *Grease* story would work in any period. It's more than just fifties nostalgia. It's really about teenage angst and the horror and wonders of being in high school. So we were looking for strong personalities that were expressed vividly through movement."

Mimi Lieber/Sauce

As Mimi recalled, "It was the first dance audition of my life. I was not a professional dancer, just a person who could dance well. We all waited in line outside the Lunt-Fontaine Theater in the Broadway district in New York for about five hours, about one thousand people. I remember I wore my trusty Levi's rolled up to the chin and some stupid argyle socks and a magenta tank top leotard, which was a combination of tough, sexy girl on the top and the lower half a boy.

"We were taught a combination which was not that hard. There were rows and rows of dancers, twenty wide, six deep. We were all doing this combination, and Pat would have the back row come forward and she would point to people and say, 'Thank you, thank you, stay.' And by the end of the day I was still there after they made their eliminations. I will never forget standing on that Broadway stage and hearing Pat Birch go down the line saying, 'Thank you, thank you,' and when she got to me, she said, 'Stay!'

"At one point we had to do things like pirouettes, so I kept making character choices. I knew because of my coloring I'd only ever be a dark 'bad' girl. So every time she'd ask me to do something I didn't know how to do, I would just stand there, cop a bad-girl attitude and say, 'I'm not going to do that!' And then she asked us all to do splits, and I couldn't get down very low, and I tried and tried to do a split, and I finally looked up at her and said, 'My character would never do the split.'

Mimi, as Sauce, is chosen to flirt with Danny during the first day of school scene.

rom paramount pictures

FOR IMMEDIATE RELEASE

April 26, 1977

HOLLYWOOD--"GREASE" will be produced by Allan Carr and Robert Stigwood for Paramount Pictures, it was announced by Michael D. Eisner, President and Chief Operating Officer of Paramount Pictures.

John Travolta will star in the Stigwood/Carr Production, which on Broadway, this past January, began its sixth year and is the sixth longest running musical in Broadway history. To date it has played 267 consecutive weeks for a total of 2,130 performances.

Travolta is currently starring in the Stigwood Production "Tribal Rites of the New Saturday Night," also for Paramount, which is based on the cover story of the same name which appeared in NEW YORK Magazine June, 1976.

Randal Kleiser will direct "GREASE" making his motion picture debut after being a successful television director. Among his credits is the highly rated telemovie for ABC-TV, "Boy In The Plastic Bubble" which also starred Travolta.

Patricia Birch will execute the choreography and m sequences for "GREASE," as she did for the original Broa Ms. Birch also served on the hit play "Candide" and cre choreography and musical sequences for the stage and f of "A Little Night Music."

(More)

Paramount A Gulf+Western Company

PARAMOUNT PICTURES CORPORATION / 5451 MARATHON ST. / HO

To Bob Goodfried
From Larry Mark

rom paramount pictures

2

FOR IMMEDIATE RELEASE

It will be lights! cameras! leather jackets and poodle skirts! when the filmmakers of "Grease" come to New York this week to cast the upcoming film version of Broadway's smash-hit musical Valentine to the Fifties.

"Grease" producers Robert Stigwood and Allan Carr, director Randal Kleiser and choreographer Patricia Birch will be auditioning dancers aged 18 to 22. The unprecedented open casting call has been scheduled for Thursday, April 28th, from 10:00 AM on at the Lunt-Fontanne Theatre, Broadway at West 46th Street.

Everyone who has ever been in any company of "Grease" and everyone who has ever wanted to be is invited to participate in the event -- provided they come dressed in Fifties costume. The proceedings promise to provide a rama-lama-ding-dong day for Fifties fanatics.

"Grease", the Stigwood-Carr Production of the hit show that started the whole Fifties craze, will be a major multi-million dollar release for Paramount Pictures.

042577

-0-

Printed in USA

Paramount A Gulf+Western Company

PARAMOUNT PICTURES CORPORATION, 1 GULF+WESTERN PLAZA, NEW YORK, N.Y. 1

And the Call Went Out!

And the second day was all couples dancing—rock 'n' roll. I had never danced like that. I had never danced touching anybody, because I grew up, you know, doing the jerk and the monkey, so it was really difficult for me. So at the end of the day, from those hundreds, there were about fourteen couples left.

"I remember going to work that night at the Bottom Line, where Tom Waits was playing. My legs were killing me—I'd never danced that much in my life. I just remember the soaring joy when Joel Thurm called our dinky apartment on the Upper West Side and told me, with this laugh in his voice, that I was coming to L.A. to make this movie. And I'd only been in New York a year from Los Angeles. So it was sort of this, you know, in my mind, this triumphant return. I went to New York to become a star—now I was coming home to be in a great movie! We got paid a big $604 a week, which at the time sounded like, I'm rich!—I'm never going to have to work again! In the twenty years since then, I've guest-starred on every show in television, I've done great movies, I've gone on national tours of Broadway shows, but I have never since been able to save the money that I saved from making that little a week. I remember I saved $11,000 and bought a car and moved back to L.A. It was great!"

Dennis Daniels/Bart

Dennis Daniels was performing in four shows a day in the Easter Show at Radio City Music Hall at the time of the open call in New York. The audition took so long he had to run back and forth from Radio City to the audition four times. He couldn't find Brylcreem to slick his hair back, so he put Vaseline in his hair instead. He said he couldn't get the Vaseline out of his hair for a week!

John Robert Garrett/Bubba

John Robert Garrett told me there were at least twelve hundred dancers at the open call in Los Angeles. It was his first film, and he remembered how high the energy was at Paramount that day. He had to wait hours to be seen, but he said it was definitely worth it!

Dennis Daniels (above), John Robert Garrett and Jennifer Buchanan (left).

Helena Androyku/Trix

Helena auditioned at the Lunt-Fontaine Theater in New York. She was twenty-one and had just spent the last year as a scholarship student with the Joffrey Ballet. She had worked with Pat before in *Music Is* . . . "I played cupid and bounced around on some trampolines." Helena and John Garrett were cast as a couple for *Grease*.

Carol Culver/Cee Cee

"I didn't audition for the *Grease* movie. By the time the movie came along, I was already assisting Pat Birch pretty regularly. I had staged the second national tour of the Broadway musical of *Grease* for her as well as having assisted her on several other projects.

"When Pat asked me to assist her on the movie, I was beside myself with excitement. I had to keep it "under wraps" since I was playing Patty Simcox at the time on Broadway, and I didn't know if anyone else in the company was going to be asked to audition for the movie.

"Allan Carr did an amazing job promoting the dance auditions on both coasts. The excitement was everywhere. I felt so privileged to be a part of something that was bound to make history. And I got to be in on everyone's auditions—all the principals as well as all the dancers. What an incredible experience to be in on all those meetings with Pat, Randal, Joel, Bronte, and Allan!"

The Girls (left) and some of the guys (right).

Barbi Alison and **Sean Moran**, both cast in New York, became the couple Midge and Moose. **Susan Susman**, born in St. Louis and cast in Los Angeles, named her character Teddy, her mother's name. **Larry Dusich**, a Californian, called himself Deuce, his nickname at UCLA, where he had originally planned to become a dentist.

Pat Birch motivated the dancers to channel their teenage ebullience into explosive, nonstop movement. The dancers kept up the pace and were tireless. They could do anything. Each of them delivered an awe-inspiring performance as the rich characters they created.

Here's a bit of *Grease* trivia—a complete list that Sean Moran found of the character names for all twenty dancers:

Helena Androyku—Trix
Antonia Franceschi—Toni
Cindy DeVore—Deana
Jennifer Buchanan—Jenny
Deborah Fishman—Babs
Sandra Gray—Big G.
Mimi Lieber—Sauce
Barbi Alison—Midge
Carol Culver—Cee Cee
Judy Susman—Teddy

Dennis Daniels—Bart
Greg Rosatti—Dego
Larry Dusich—Deuce
John Robert Garrett—Bubba
Andy Roth—Eddie
Richard Weisman—Buz
Lou Spadaccini—Woppo
Sean Moran—Moose
Daniel Levans—St.Vitus
Andy Tennant—Arnold

Without a doubt, the dancers were the heartbeat of the movie. Their energy and talent inspired everyone around them, and they made the rest of us look good. They are one of the main reasons that *Grease* sparkles.

And that's how the movie got cast!

Mimi Lieber, Antonia Franceschi, Sandra Gray, and Deborah Fishman (above). Judy Susman and Andy Tennant (right).

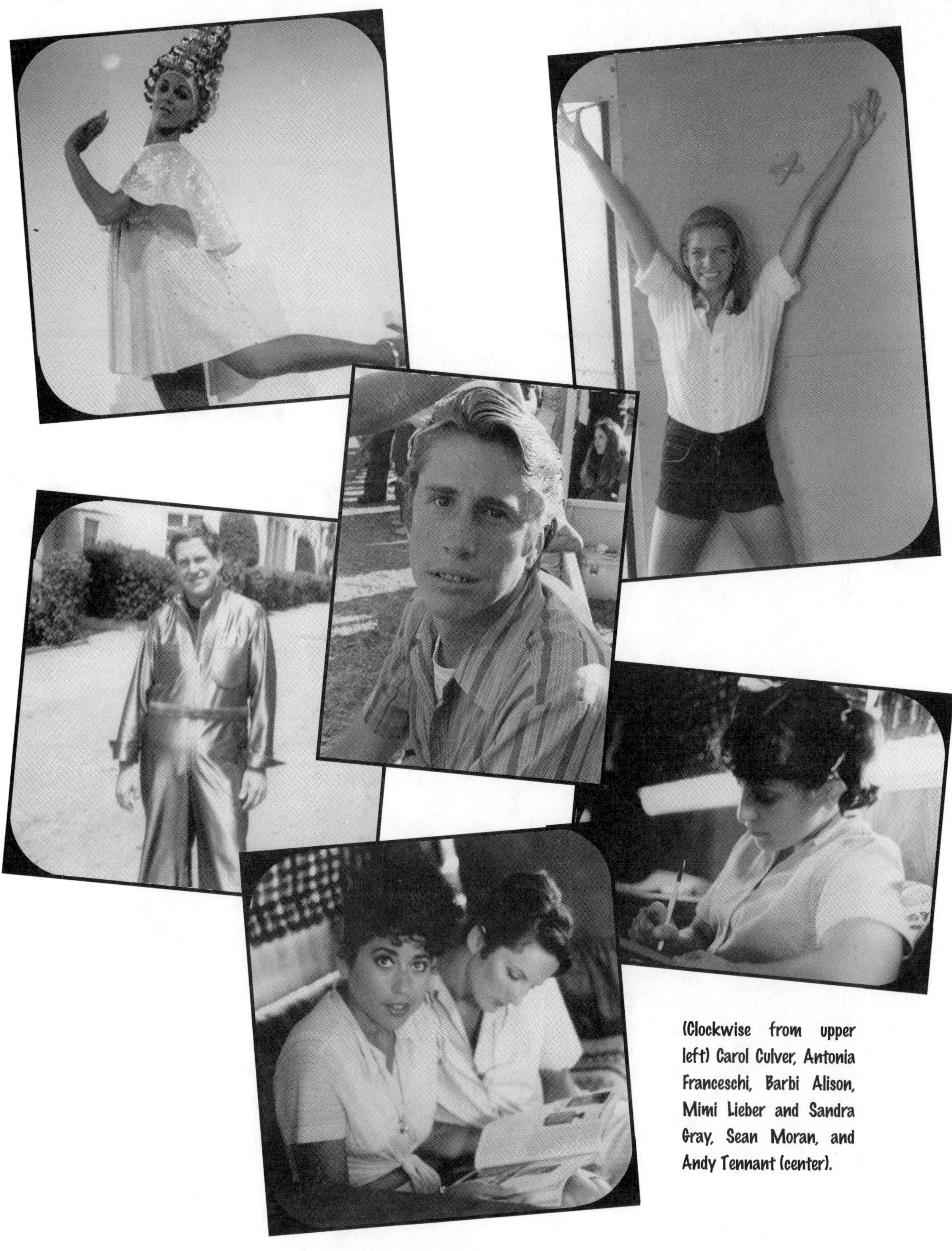

(Clockwise from upper left) Carol Culver, Antonia Franceschi, Barbi Alison, Mimi Lieber and Sandra Gray, Sean Moran, and Andy Tennant (center).

(Clockwise from upper left) Mimi Lieber, Sandra Gray, Antonia Franceschi and Helena Androyku, Dennis Daniels, John Robert Garrett and Dennis Daniels, and Pat Birch (center).

THAT WAS THEN

Rehearsals

Kelly, Olivia, Michael, me, Barry, and Pat Birch taking a "break" from rehearsals.

Three weeks prior to filming, the whole cast assembled in the old commissary at Paramount to rehearse all the musical numbers and scenes. Three weeks is an unusually long rehearsal period for a movie, but musicals take a lot more preparation than normal films. Every morning we would separate into groups. Some of us would rehearse scenes, others would be learning music, and still others would be tackling new dance steps. Dennis Daniels and Carol Culver, Pat Birch's assistants, would teach us some basic steps and then encourage us to take the time to explore how our characters would interpret these new moves. This was a time of discovery for all of us. I must admit some of us were a *little* bit older than the characters we were hired to play, so we used the rehearsal time to immerse ourselves in the feelings and desires of seniors in high school.

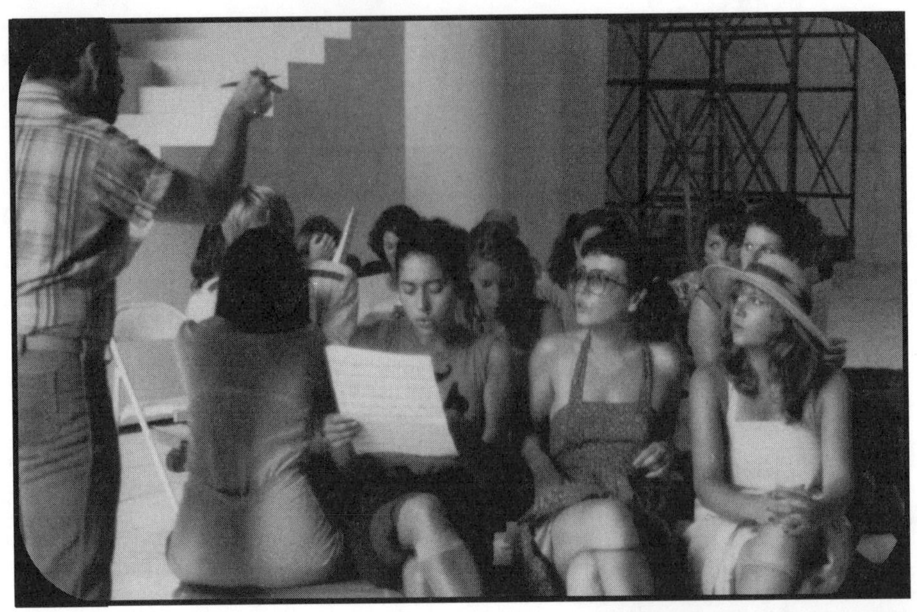

Mimi, Jamie (pigtails) and Dinah (straw hat) paying close attention to Louis St. Louis (above). Stockard Channing practices looking uninterested, while Susan Buckner (Patty Simcox) and I are enthralled (right). "Met a boy, cute as can be" (below).

At the end of the three weeks, we performed all the musical numbers for the chief executives at Paramount. In his letter to them, Allan suggested that the staff use their discretion in telling the actors about the importance of this presentation. I think he was afraid that if the actors knew that all the chief executives of Paramount were going to be watching them, they would be too nervous and screw up!

Of course, we all knew whom we were performing for that day. We were so psyched and proud of how hard we had worked that we gave a fantastic presentation. There were some well-known movie stars there, too. I remember Barry Pearl's jaw hitting the floor when he saw his all-time favorite actor, Jack Nicholson, in the audience. Warren Beatty, who was shooting *Heaven Can Wait* next door, was there, too, which had a similar effect on *my* jaw.

INTER-COMMUNICATION

TO: ALL STAFF

DATE: June 17, 1977

FROM: ALLAN CARR

SUBJECT: "GREASE"

At the request of Barry Diller, Paramount Pictures is flying out the entire New York Executive Staff, including Gordon Weaver, Vice President of Advertising and Promotion, etc., as well as several very important exhibitors representing some very large movie chains on Wednesday, June 22. We will be giving them a "sneak preview" of our music numbers. This event will start at 11:30 a.m. followed by cocktails and lunch on the set. We are requesting all our cameos to make an appearance, even if they are not working on that day. I will discuss all the specifics with Pat Birch.

However, this is a very, very important day for us and we want to put our best dancing foot forward!

Allan Carr
ALLAN CARR

P.S. It's late Friday afternoon, please no comments about spelling or literary content of this memo.

P.P.S. Pat, at your discretion, please notify members of our cast.

A memo from The Boss.

On the Set Memories

The first day of shooting, June 23, 1977

During the telephone interviews I conducted to gather material for this book, I asked everyone what their most vivid memories of the shooting period were. I learned many interesting things, like how they prepared for and approached their roles, and what led to some great bits of improvised business that weren't in the script. It was inevitable that such spontaneous behavior would emerge when we were in front of the camera, because the intensity of our belief in the story was so great and we were having so much fun playing with each other. Also, our director, Randal, was without a doubt our best audience.

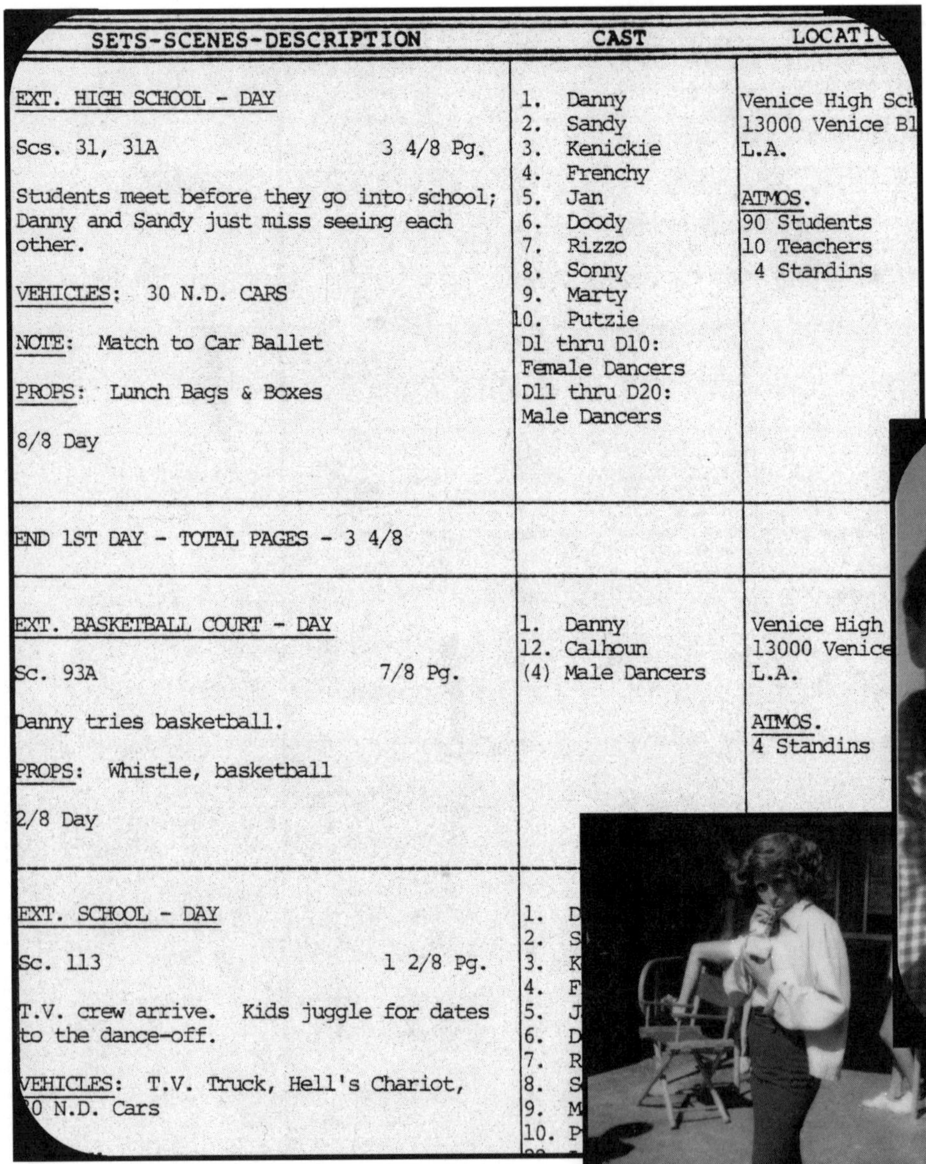

SETS-SCENES-DESCRIPTION	CAST	LOCATI
EXT. HIGH SCHOOL - DAY Scs. 31, 31A 3 4/8 Pg. Students meet before they go into school; Danny and Sandy just miss seeing each other. VEHICLES: 30 N.D. CARS NOTE: Match to Car Ballet PROPS: Lunch Bags & Boxes 8/8 Day	1. Danny 2. Sandy 3. Kenickie 4. Frenchy 5. Jan 6. Doody 7. Rizzo 8. Sonny 9. Marty 10. Putzie D1 thru D10: Female Dancers D11 thru D20: Male Dancers	Venice High Sch 13000 Venice Bl L.A. ATMOS. 90 Students 10 Teachers 4 Standins
END 1ST DAY - TOTAL PAGES - 3 4/8		
EXT. BASKETBALL COURT - DAY Sc. 93A 7/8 Pg. Danny tries basketball. PROPS: Whistle, basketball 2/8 Day	1. Danny 12. Calhoun (4) Male Dancers	Venice High 13000 Venice L.A. ATMOS. 4 Standins
EXT. SCHOOL - DAY Sc. 113 1 2/8 Pg. T.V. crew arrive. Kids juggle for dates to the dance-off. VEHICLES: T.V. Truck, Hell's Chariot, 0 N.D. Cars	1. D 2. S 3. K 4. F 5. J 6. D 7. R 8. S 9. M 10. P	

The production schedule for the first day of shooting (the movie was filmed in 53 days) (above). Me and my boyfriend, Doody (top). Me and 'Liv (middle). Pat Birch as Dinah's temporary stand-in (right).

The First Kiss

The opening scene of *Grease* is very tender and romantic. Sandy and Danny are alone on a deserted beach, taking photos, playing in the surf and chasing each other around until finally things lead to their first kiss. At the time, John and Olivia were still almost strangers, so I had to ask Olivia something I was always dying to know: How was that first kiss with John?

"It was lovely," she says. "He's so beautiful. But I have to tell you, I was very worried about the tide. I was sure we were going to get dumped by the waves."

Of course, I had to ask John the same question!

"Well, you know it was wonderful for me," he says, "because I got to kiss her and it was all within the rules. You know, even if you dated someone like Olivia, God, who knows when you'd get to the first kiss. Imagine being within the rules and you're able to do it right away! It was quite a fantastic feeling."

"'Love' is a many splendored thing. . . ."

Summer Nights

Now remember, Pat Birch choreographed the original Broadway play, so she had a pretty good idea how she wanted this number to translate to film. For rehearsal and the Paramount presentation, the boys and the girls were right next to each other—the way the number had been performed on the stage. However, when we were filming, the boys shot their section first and separately on the bleachers of the football field at Venice High School, in Venice, California.

The temperature was in the high nineties the week we filmed that number. As John explains: "I don't know about you girls, but 'Summer Nights' was really hot to film. I'm not just referring to the temperature. It was the first day of filming and we were all fired up. I loved that number. But we were all in leather jackets and we were drenched with sweat."

We girls rehearsed our part of "Summer Nights" at the outdoor cafeteria while the guys were shooting theirs at the football field. During our break, we would sneak over behind the bleachers to watch how they were doing. The prerecorded musical tracks were blaring over the outdoor P.A. system, and those boys were really cooking!

Watching the guys really turned us on and when the camera was focused on us, we were psyched and ready to jump all over those picnic tables and plead with Sandy to tell us more!

Susan Buckner, who played Patty Simcox, told me "Summer Nights" was her favorite musical number. "I loved the freedom we all had to improvise and come up with ideas. I think it was my idea to fall over the garbage can after Rizzo tripped me. I love all that physical stuff. I really wanted to dive into the can head first with my feet waving in the air, but Randal thought I might break my neck. I didn't care. I thought, What the heck, at least they would have the shot!"

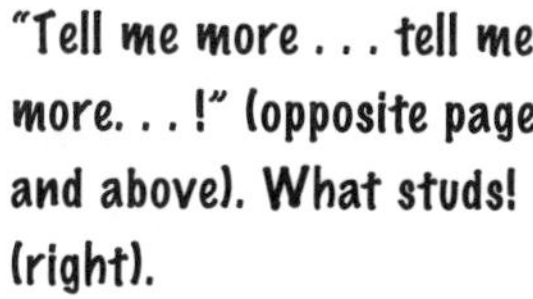

"Tell me more . . . tell me more. . . !" (opposite page and above). What studs! (right).

Pat gives John some tips as Randal looks on (top). The T-Birds (middle and bottom).

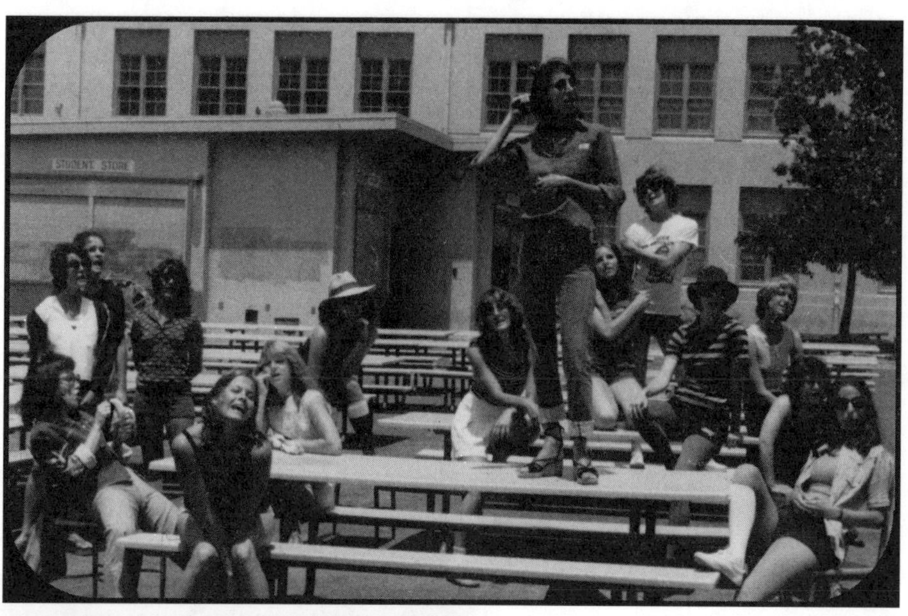

Rehearsing at Venice High (top), "Oh, those Summer Nights" (middle), "We stayed out 'til ten o'clock. . . ." (bottom).

Rydell High

Olivia and I made our first entrance together walking to Rydell on the first day of school. Sandy is frightened and insecure. She feels like an outsider starting at a new school in her senior year. We decided that Sandy and Frenchy live next door to each other, and Frenchy has become very protective of Sandy.

While we were waiting to shoot our little scene, I asked Olivia how Rydell differed from the high school she went to in Australia. "It was totally different. I went to University High School in Melbourne," she said. "First of all, we had to wear uniforms. Second, the boys and girls were segregated. They had a boys' end of the school and a girls' end and a boys' eating area and a girls' eating area. You only saw the boys in class and at school functions or assembly. Basically, it was very strict, and you had to wear your hat and your gloves home, and they'd check you to make sure your uniforms were the right length and all that. And that was a *public* high school. But all the schools in Australia required the students to wear uniforms, so it was very, very different from Rydell."

I asked Michael Tucci about the Italian curse he muttered behind Principal McGee's back. "That was all improvised," he confirms. "I wanted to say 'Fongool!,'' but Allan said I couldn't because Stockard was saying it at the end of 'Look At Me, I'm Sandra Dee.' I begged him to let me say it. Sonny always says that—it's his favorite expression. When the camera was rolling, when McGee wasn't looking at me, I put in the phrase 'A fanable tutti putana.' Allan had to check out what it meant

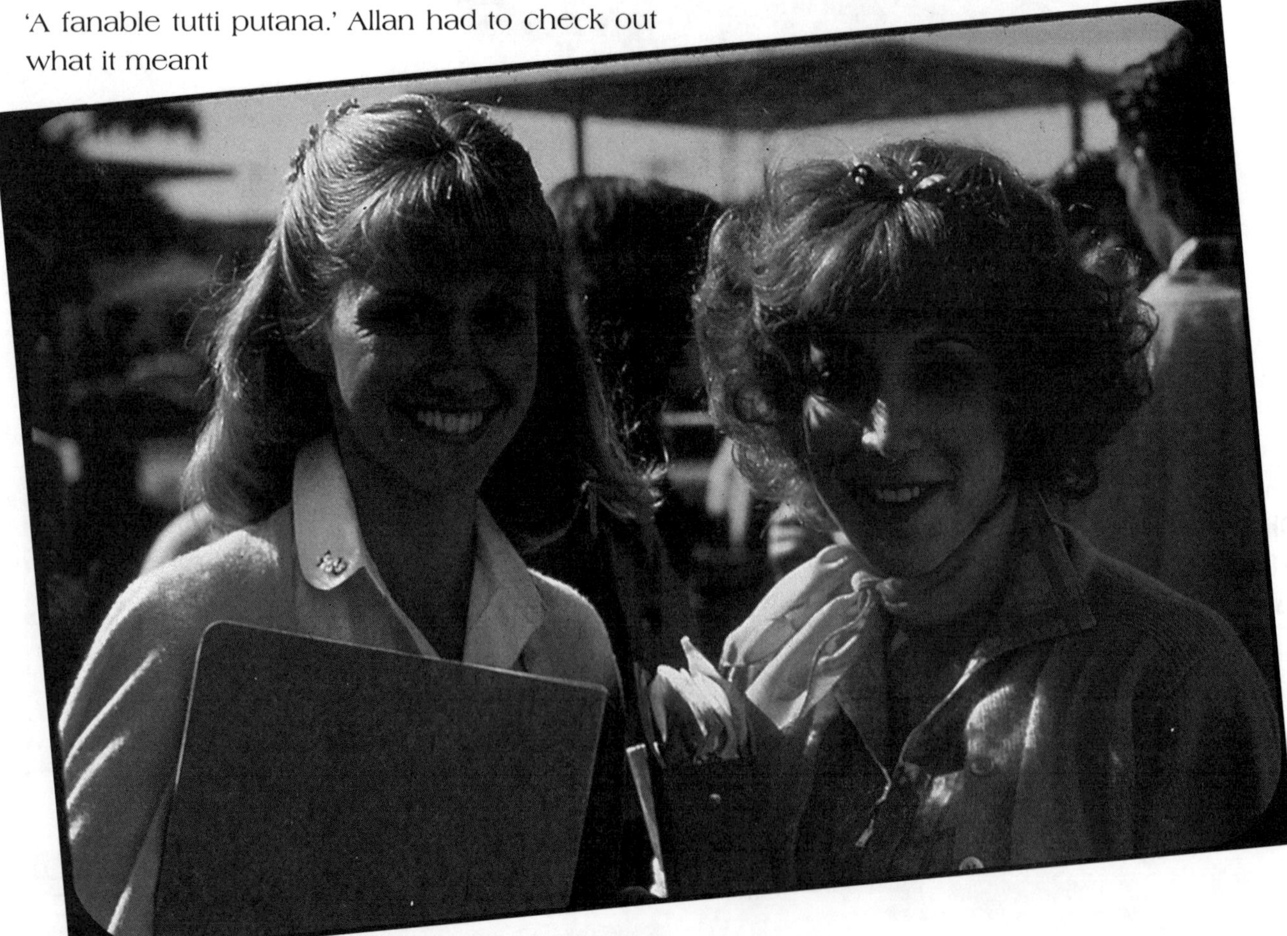

before he would use it in the movie. I had my Aunt Zizi translate it for him. She said it meant 'May all the bad girls go to Naples.' It really means something much dirtier; literally it means 'May all the whores go to Naples.' So I called the principal a whore and they kept it in the movie."

Danny Zuko's homeroom class was in the biology lab, and Randal Kleiser wanted John to play around with a frog. Randal tells me, "I wanted Danny to say, 'Plunk your magic twanger, Froggy'—which was from the Andy Devine television show that I thought Baby Boomers would remember—and pick up a frog that was just dissected and dance it around. But everyone thought that no one would know that television show, so they made me cut it out."

Around the second week of filming, my youngest brother Richard came to visit me on location at Venice High School. He was ten at the time and idolized John Travolta. He wanted to *be* John Travolta! He played Danny Zuko in camp the summer before we shot the movie. When he came to visit me on the set, he asked me if I would bring him to John's trailer so that he could meet him privately. When I told him of course, he said he'd be right back. Then he disappeared. It turned out he went to my hairdresser on the film and asked her if she could slick back his hair to look like John's. Then he was ready to meet his idol.

When I brought him into John's Winnebago, he said hello and shook his hand and then started to dance all over and sing "Greased Lightnin'." I must say, he was adorable, and John really liked him. In fact, after we finished shooting that day, John asked me if we had ever been to Disneyland. We hadn't, so John said, "Why don't I take you both there tonight."

So there we were in our first stretch limo going to Disneyland. John told us we would not have a good time if he got recognized, so he instructed us not to call him by his name. In fact, when we arrived there, we went directly to Frontierland and he bought a disguise—sunglasses and a Daniel Boone hat. We called him Uncle Bob, and he went unnoticed for about an hour.

Then a large group of teenage girls started to point in our direction and whisper to each other. We looked for a way to escape but they were gaining on us. John said, "Uh oh, don't look now, but I think I've been spotted." Sure enough, the group of girls started giggling and moving very quickly toward us, and when they got right in front, one said, "Aren't you . . . the girl from *You Light Up My Life*?" I meekly said, "Yes," signed some autographs, grabbed my brother's arm with one hand and "Uncle Bob's" arm with the other, and as we hurried away we all had a good laugh. My little brother is now thirty-one years old—and a fantastic singer. In fact, he made his Metropolitan Opera debut two years ago!

Who knew?!!!

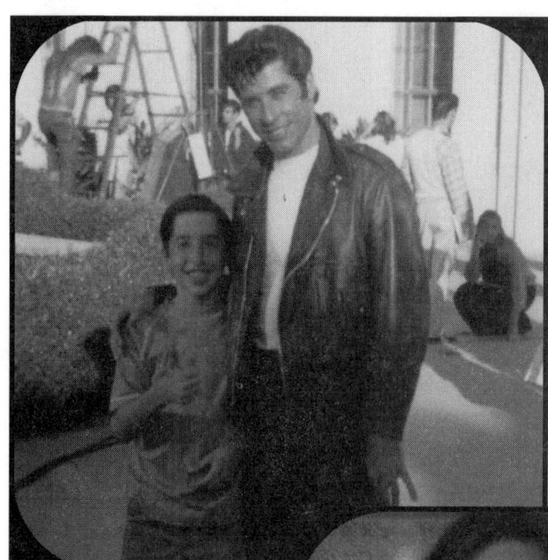

My little brother Richard Bernstein with John (above) and with me (right).

The Pep Rally

On an actor's resumé there is usually a section called "special skills." This can include such things as proficiency in a sport or musical instrument or a talent for speaking foreign languages or dialects. The incomparable dancer Dennis Daniels, who named his character Bart, was the 1974–1975 United States World Baton champion. The pep rally, our first night shoot, started shooting on a Monday night. During rehearsal, the Friday before, Dennis was asked if he could twirl fire batons at the pep rally. Here's what Dennis remembers:

Sandy gets a glimpse of Tom (below), the T-Birds and the Pink Ladies looking too cool for school at the pep rally (right).

"Pat Birch said, 'Dennis can twirl fire batons!' I loved that. It was kind of off the top of her head. She forgot about the fact that I didn't have any equipment. No one had fire equipment in Los Angeles. I called my brother Michael in St. Louis, Missouri, and he rushed over to my apartment there. He found my equipment but it was Friday and we needed it by Monday. So Paramount flew my brother to Los Angeles on two minutes' notice, which cost them a lot of money. He actually helped me with all the prep work during filming and has a cameo appearance in the movie, plus he had this two-week paid vacation in California. It was really fun."

During a closeup of Tom Chisum, played by Lorenzo Lamas, looking at Sandy at the pep rally, Lorenzo improvised mouthing "Hi!" and "How are you?" to Sandy. When it was time for Olivia's closeup, she answered him and mouthed "Fine" back. It was not in the script, but they kept it in. So Lorenzo, who had no lines in the actual script, wound up with two lines in the finished movie. Clever guy.

Barry Pearl had an inspired idea at the pep rally. He felt Doody was definitely a Three Stooges fan, so he choreographed one of the classic Three Stooges routines for Sonny, Putzie, and Doody. It was a perfect bit of "business" for the guys, and Randal loved it and kept it in the movie.

"Danny?!" "Sandy?!"

Look At Me, I'm Sandra Dee

Frenchy is really Sandy's only friend. She knows Sandy feels terrible about Danny's strange behavior and she wants to cheer her up. So Frenchy invites her for a "night out" with the girls.

Filming the sleepover scene in Frenchy's bedroom was a riot. We were not on location in a real bedroom but on a soundstage. There were fifty or sixty crew members all focused on the scene we were about to film. But once we were in our pajamas and hair rollers and walked onto the set, we felt like we were totally alone, and we all simultaneously got the giggles! We were exploding with high energy and teenage horniness. We all carried on so much, laughing and tickling, that Randal thought we wouldn't be able to focus on our lines. But we all knew that when he said "action" we would channel all that youthful vitality into the scene. I was so into my role that when Rizzo pulled out the bottle of wine, I spontaneously leaped off my bed and closed my bedroom door so that my "parents" wouldn't hear us!

When I think of Jamie Donnelly as Jan, I see a good girl who behind closed doors could be really bad! She was always making us all laugh by imitating people. I wondered how Jamie would describe Jan.

"I always felt she was a person whose identity was through her relationship to the group. Being a Pink Lady made her feel important. She was an insecure person, a little on the chubby side, and she wasn't that beautiful and didn't feel like she was that smart. But she had great friends, and everything good that happened to her was because of her relationship with the Pink Ladies."

"I'm no object of lust (not!)."

At the top the scene, Jan was supposed to be watching television, and then Loretta Young comes on the screen. Her line was "Look at what Loretta Young is wearing." That was the way it was in the script, but I was pretty sure it was Jamie's idea to change it.

"Yeah, I had that line which I felt referred to something Jan wouldn't care about. I don't think Jan knew who Loretta Young *was*! I asked Randal if we could replace it with something else, and Randal asked me what I had in mind. I remembered a line in the original show that referred to Bucky Beaver. Someone looked at me in the play and said, 'No s—, Bucky Beaver.' I remember it getting a good laugh in the show, but Bucky Beaver was nowhere to be found in the screenplay.

"I went and asked Randal what he thought, and he said, 'Well, how would we do it?' And I said, 'Well, you got to get the Ipana toothpaste commercials from the fifties of Bucky Beaver and put it on the TV, and then I'll imitate the beaver.' And he said, 'Jamie, we'll get it for you, but I don't know whether it will work—you have to show it to me.' So because it was Paramount and they could get anything, they got me two commercials of Bucky Beaver, and I looked at them and showed them to the rest of the girls, and we all laughed and said, 'We got to show Randal, we got to show Randal!' And Randal came over and said, 'Okay, fine, let's try it, let's use it, let's do it.' And that's how it wound up in there. I'm really glad I spoke up."

"Brusha, brusha, brusha!"

Olivia sings a John Farrar classic.

Hopelessly Devoted to You

At the conclusion of "Look At Me, I'm Sandra Dee," Sandy is feeling very hurt because her new friends have just made fun of her. Allan Carr thought that Sandy should have a song to sing at such an emotional moment. So Olivia called a dear friend, songwriter John Farrar, to ask him to take a shot at writing a ballad for Sandy.

John, who had produced Olivia's albums and her platinum single "I Honestly Love You," and who wrote, arranged, and produced her smash hit "Have You Never Been Mellow," read the script and had an idea. "Do you remember that beautiful Skeeter Davis song, 'The End of the World?'" John asked me when I interviewed him. "You know, 'Why does my heart go on beating . . .' Well, that's the feel I was looking for. . . ." John was sitting on the floor in Allan's office when Allan walked in and said, "You must be the songwriter!" "Why," queried John, "Do all writers sit on the floor?" Allan laughed and told John that he loved "Hopelessly Devoted to You" and that he was going to put it into the movie.

Greased Lightnin'

Twenty years is a long time, and believe me, I needed a little help to jog my memory. No one better for that than Joel Thurm. Not only did he cast the movie brilliantly, but it was his idea for Danny Zuko to sing "Greased Lightnin'," the song that Kenickie sings in the original play. Joel had produced a film called *Boy in the Plastic Bubble* and brought together Randal Kleiser, its director, with John Travolta, its star. So there was a very strong connection among the three of them.

I loved "Greased Lightnin'." I asked John if it was his idea to dance around the car with the Saran Wrap.

> "No," John said, "that was from the play. It was just kind of roughly thrown around in the play, and it got a big laugh. In the movie, when we ran around the car with it, we used it like a musical instrument. I don't think the kids who see the movie now know what it really was about. I mean, in the play, the Saran Wrap was used instead of a prophylactic. In the movie, I think kids just think it's some leftover shopping thing. The only way to get it in the movie was to use it as a prop or something, and, in theory, it made a bigger moment of it.

The Saran Wrap Moment.

"Go Greased Lightnin'!!"

"It wasn't any different than that moment with Dinah Manoff and Edd Byrnes, when she tells Vince her name is 'Maraschino . . . like the cherry.' I mean, that was so dirty and erotic, but it passed over all the kids' heads just like the Saran Wrap did. Those moments are actually raunchier than everyone pretends they are, especially when very young kids are going to be watching."

Our patient and resourceful property master, Richard Valesko, told me that there were over 264 tires used in the "Greased Lightnin'" fantasy number. Twenty-four of those tires were painted white, and four of them are the oversize tires which are used on the fantasy car itself. Greased Lightnin', Kenickie's actual car, is really four cars in all—with five motors. There's the car used before the T-Birds get to it, the two used for the race at Thunder Road, and the fantasy car, which has one shiny dummy engine for the musical number and another real one, which drove the film's stars to *Grease* premieres around the world.

Kelly, Olivia, and Dennis Daniels ("Is she hot or what?" asks Dennis) (above), "Greased Lightnin'," the trading card (right).

The Frosty Palace

I always wanted to be an actress, except for maybe five minutes in junior high when I wanted to be an astronaut. So I could relate to Frenchy's unrelenting drive to become a beautician. But since I had never aspired to be a hairdresser, my first research project, as I prepared to play Frenchy, was to go to two different Los Angeles beauty schools and see what their curricula were. I sure was surprised. There was much more to beauty school than I had ever imagined. I actually kept the page of notes I wrote before filming began, in which I analyze what I felt Frenchy's thoughts about herself were, and also describe the differences between the two beauty schools I visited.

BEAUTY SCHOOLS

1. John Robert Powers.
I am a careerist. I am interested in career advancement. One of my hobbies is reading fan and glamour magazines. I also collect gum wrappers. I must devote 4 to 5 hours every day to the above. Oh yeah I also enjoy playing records that are hits. I would like to concentrate on the following areas in my training. Hair is numero uno! Next would be Assurance and Poise. My main goal is to learn all I can about hair. I would like to learn to do all the basic styles and to invent some of my own. I would like to have my own shop someday.
this school features courses in:
travelling wardrobe 1. WARDROBE - what colors look better
2. POISE - LEARNING TO WALK - getting in and out of CARS.
3. Shapes of earrings
4. Voice - project who you are through your voice
5. Personality Development - your assets and liabilities
6 The MAN OF YOUR DREAMS
7. GOOD MANNERS - at PARTIES or expensive restaurants
SAT. 1-2 Communication.

When we rehearsed the scene that precedes "Beauty School Dropout," with all the Pink Ladies and T-birds crunched together around the booth at the Frosty Palace, Stockard practiced throwing the milkshake at Jeff with an empty glass. The idea was that the strawberry milkshake would miss him and hit me instead. It was important that the milkshake got all over *me*, because that was my moti-

After eight takes, bingo!

vation for taking off the scarf that was covering my pink hair. But when the cameras were rolling and Stockard was armed with a big, full glass of pink milkshake, she kept missing me and hitting Jeff, bull's-eye, right in the face.

We did take two. Again Stockard missed me completely and got the milkshake all over Jeff. On the next take, I moved a little bit closer to him so that maybe I would get some milkshake remnants on me on the rebound. No such luck. Stockard would fling that milkshake in my direction and I wouldn't even get a drop of it on me. Jeff remembers how it felt to get milkshake all over him:

> "We must have shot that scene seven or eight times before Stockard missed me and got you. After every take I had to change my clothes and get washed up and start all over again. I don't know whether you even know this, but six months later, in December, Stockard and I shot a scene that is not in the movie, where the milkshake has already been thrown and we are outside the Frosty Palace. It was really intense. I'm standing there covered with pink milkshake, and we're yelling at each other like Stanley and Stella in *A Streetcar Named Desire*. I heard that Michael Eisner and Robert Stigwood wanted the scene to stay in the movie, but Allan Carr didn't because he thought it was too heavy."

I asked Randal Kleiser if he thought that scene would be in the re-released version of the movie. "There was a reason why we cut it out," he said emphatically, "but now there is so much interest in it that a lot of people probably would like to see it as a curiosity."

Beauty School Dropout

Rehearsals for Beauty School Dropout (above and right).

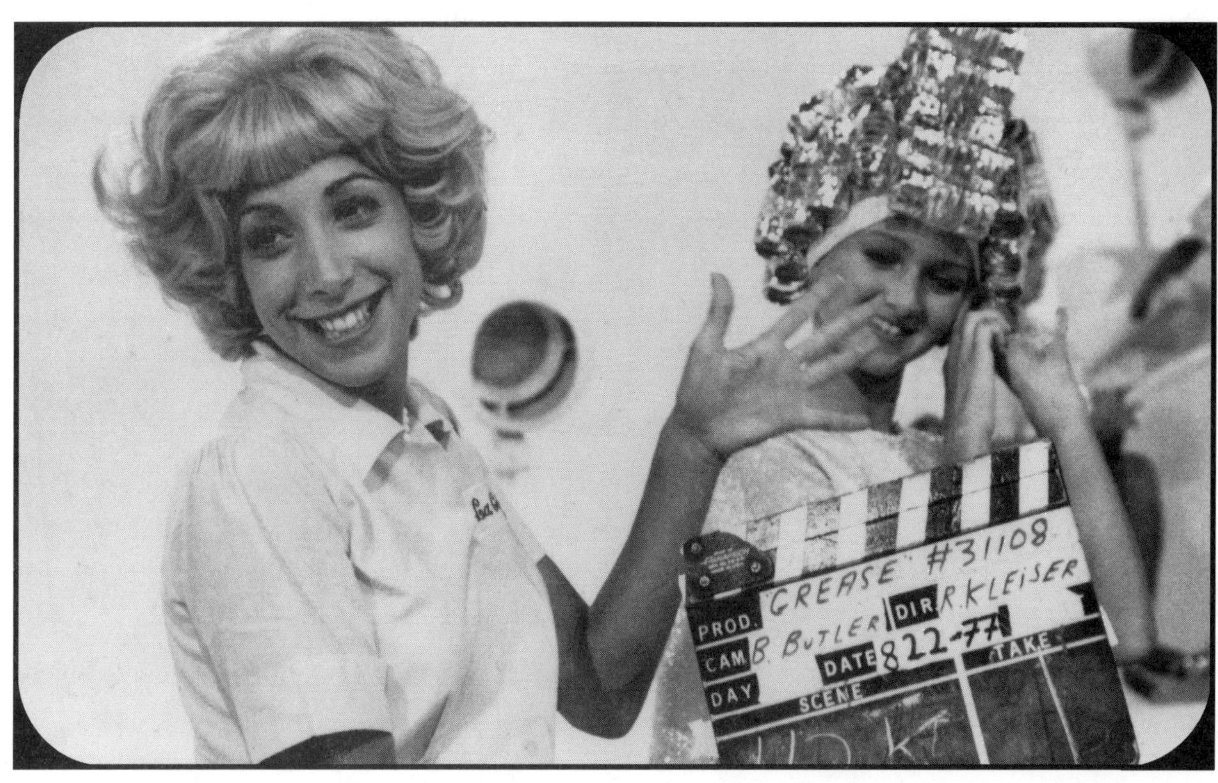

The first time I called Frankie Avalon to interview him for this book, he wasn't home and I got a big kick out of hearing his voice on his answering machine. I hadn't seen him or spoken to him since we shot our scene so many years before. I called him again the next day; this time he answered the phone, I told him it was Frenchy, and he started to laugh.

He told me that "Beauty School Dropout" is probably his most popular song! "What is amazing, Didi," he said, "is that I had so many hit records in my career, and 'Venus' used to be the biggest one of all time, but because of the movie of *Grease*, there are now several generations that know and love 'Beauty School Dropout.' Don't forget that the sound track sold over twenty-five million albums."

Frankie was surprised when I told him something he never knew before—that "Beauty School Dropout" was the first song written for *Grease*. Jim Jacobs, one of the creators of the original Broadway musical, told me how Warren Casey, his late collaborator, got the idea for the song:

> "Well, the way it happened was, Warren was over at my house one time, years before the idea of *Grease* ever came up, and I had the TV on late one night. These three gang guys in Chicago had murdered a man who had gone out to get a package of cigarettes, and they broadcast this on the news and showed these three juvenile delinquents.
>
> "They had caught the three punks, and they were describing that one guy was sixteen, one worked for a construction firm and he was eighteen years old, and another guy had dropped out of high school and had gone to beauty school but had dropped out! I turned to Warren and I said, 'Man, can you imagine anything lower than a beauty school dropout?' And Warren just laughed hysterically.

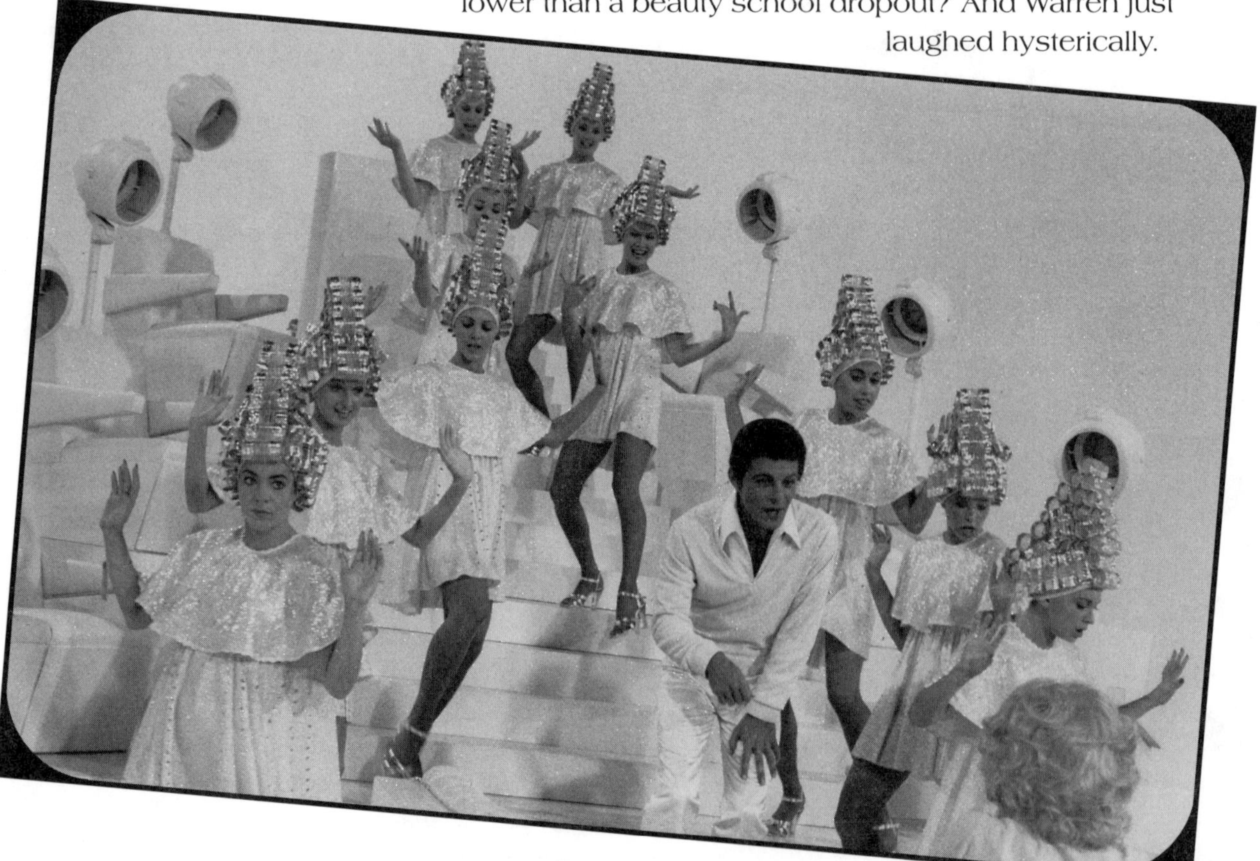

TEEN ANGEL
(continuing;
singing)
A teen-age ne'er-do-well
Most mixed-up non-delinquent on
the block
Your future's so unclear now
What's left of your career now?
Can't even get a trade-in on
your smock.

Beauty School dropout
No graduation day for you
Beauty School dropout
Missed your midterms and flunked
shampoo

Well, at least you could have
taken time
To wash and clean your clothes up
After spending all that dough to
have
The doctor fix your nose up
Baby, get movin'
Why keep the feeble hopes alive?
What are you provin'?
You got the dream but not the
drive
If you go for your diploma you
could join a steno pool
Turn in your teasing comb and go
back to high school.

Beauty School dropout
Hangin' around the corner store
Beauty School dropout
It is about time you knew the
score.

Well, they couldn't teach you
anything
You think you're such a looker
But no customer would go to you
Unless she was a hooker.
(MORE)

(CONTINUED)

It was one of the best days of my life!

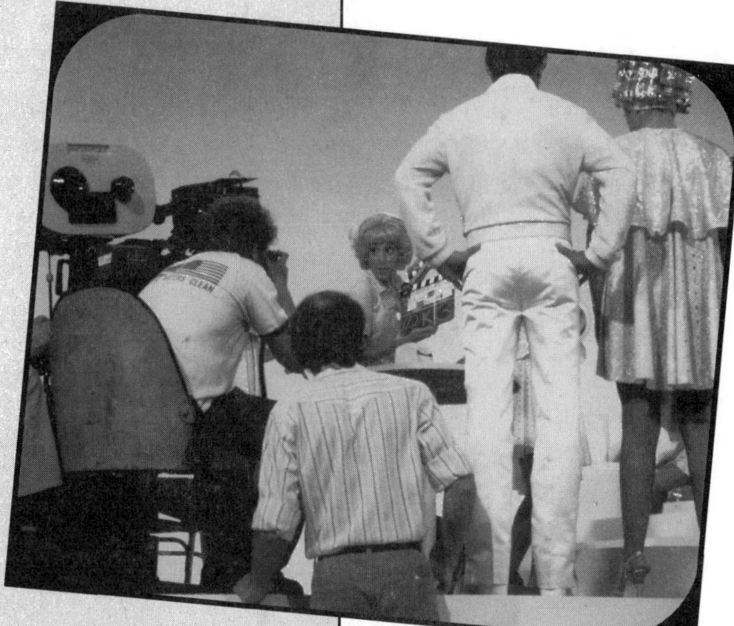

"Then, unbeknownst to me, he went and wrote the song during the course of the next week and came over and played it. That was why the intro line was 'most mixed up nondelinquent on the block,' because they categorized these guys as juvenile delinquents. 'Beauty School Dropout' was actually written about this Italian kid in Chicago who had been accused of murder! And it was such a good song that when we were writing *Grease* I said we had to figure out a way to get it in."

How do you like that?! I can't tell you what a thrill it was to have two full days devoted to shooting my character's fantasy.

I had a wonderful friend and drama coach at that time, Mr. Edmund Pardo, and we had lots of fun working on *Grease*. We spent a long time preparing for this scene. We studied how it builds from the shame Frenchy feels for failing tinting class, to her deciding to drop out of beauty school, to her wishing she had a guardian angel to advise her how to handle the shock of her wish coming true. When I got dressed in my La Coiffure uniform and they put the pink wig on me, I looked in the mirror and thought, I better forget everything we worked on. I look bizarre enough with that pink hair, and if I try to do anything funny on top of it, it will be too much.

I immediately called Mr. Pardo and told him how I felt. He thought I was only getting cold feet and said, "As soon as you break for lunch you better drive right over here." Luckily, we rehearsed for the camera all morning and didn't film anything. As soon as we broke, I jumped in my car and drove west to Beverly Hills for the emergency meeting. On my way, stopping for a light, I looked to my left, and a car full of guys were pointing and laughing at me. I couldn't understand why, and then I looked in my rearview mirror and realized I was driving around with pink hair! I had forgotten how weird I looked. (Remember, this was before "punk" became fashionable.) But I had no time to be embarrassed. I ran up the stairs to Mr. Pardo's apartment, he took one look at me and cracked up. We went over the lyric of "Beauty School Dropout," and he agreed I should do as little as possible.

In fact, I didn't have to do anything in that scene but look at Frankie Avalon. Even though he was singing lyrics like, "You think you're such a looker/But no customer would go to you unless she was a hooker!" he was so gorgeous I couldn't help drooling!

And about those "angels" that fly over my head at the end, Barry Pearl tells me,

"First of all, not only were we high, we were very high—if you get my drift. I thought I would love flying in as an angel at the end of your fantasy sequence, but I didn't enjoy it nearly as much as I had hoped. They had us wear these makeshift harnesses over our jeans that were not constructed properly and were cut off right under the crotch. They put lamb fleece in the jeans to pad the area, but it was so tight that my crotch went numb. Also, if that wasn't scary enough, they kept us hanging up there for hours. It seemed like it took forever for them to shoot that scene."

Well, Barry, maybe it felt like it took forever for you, but I could have spent an eternity staring into Frankie's big brown eyes!

Randal also told me something of interest to technophile trivia buffs. He was pretty sure that the special effects around my face when I look up at Frankie Avalon in the number were created by computer graphics for the first time in a movie. And the colorful lights around Frankie were also done using the same process.

Poor Michael not only had a numb crotch, they couldn't get him down. His rope was stuck on one of the beams.

Finally someone brought in a big ladder and rescued him.

The Dance-Off

The sound tracks for musical films are almost always prerecorded. That is to say, the music tracks, both instrumental and vocal, are recorded in a recording studio before the shooting of the musical numbers takes place, and then, during the filming, the performers lip-synch to the recorded tracks. This allows for a clarity and accuracy of recording that would be impossible to achieve if the vocals had to be recorded while the performers were moving around and dancing during the shooting. My first brush with this fascinating process was when I made *You Light Up My Life*, a movie about a pop singer whom I portrayed. But with its big singing cast, many ensemble vocals and huge dance sequences, the prerecords for *Grease* were a much more elaborate and complicated undertaking—and a lot more fun.

Jamie, me, and Dinah in the recording studio (left). Kelly, Jeff, Barry, and Michael (right).

Danny McBride was the lead guitarist with Sha Na Na, the popular group that was cast as the band that played for the dance-off, and he gives a more detailed look at the prerecord process:

"We were in production on our TV series when we found out *Grease* would be shooting in and around Los Angeles, which was perfect because we did the TV show there in the heart of Hollywood. We did the prerecorded music tracks with Charles Fox, the musical director at the time, on the Paramount lot (also in the middle of Hollywood) at the fabulous Glen Glenn Studios. You could record a hundred-piece orchestra in there, and here we were—piano, guitar, sax, bass, and drums, with a few singers. What a place!

The fabulous Sha Na Na.

"Prerecorded tracks are necessary in film and television for dancers to practice with. That way, the music is exactly the same every time, not a beat faster or slower, so dance rehearsals run smoothly. Think of the prom scene—the many dance steps, moves, twists, lifts, spins, etcetera. To make sure the music fit everything she had in mind, Pat Birch came to the recording sessions and stood, or rather did little steps, in the control room. Faster . . . or slower, she would suggest to Charlie Fox, and then we would put down on tape just what she wanted. Filmmaking sure is a collaborative process."

Danny's recollections of life on the set are also fascinating.

"I remember it being a complete shock to my body clock the first day we were required on the set to film what turned out to be the first of several days of filming. We were needed in wardrobe and makeup at something like six A.M. That's normally bedtime for rock musicians. So this was one part of moviemaking that came as a rude awakening—literally. And everyone was always so chipper and perky, all the cast and crew, except me—I was a growly bear. I soon realized that hanging with the old pros and listening to their stories made it all worthwhile. Moviemaking is a lot of hurry up and wait—while they set lights, focal lengths for cameras, rewire a line for sound, fix a piece of wardrobe or a hairstyle, or a hundred other things so everything looks right on screen. Eve Arden, Alice Ghostley, Sid Caesar—these people were showbiz royalty to me, and to hang out and listen and kibitz was a rare treat. *Our Miss Brooks* in person! And Sid Caesar: a comedy god. I had also been a fan of *77 Sunset Strip* and, when I was a kid, owned a copy of 'Kookie, Kookie, Lend Me Your Comb,' Edd Byrnes's huge 1959 smash. He was too cool."

Danny added one more note of crucial importance. "We've all taken turns over the years arguing jokingly which one of us was actually Johnny Casino. I can settle that here once and for all—*I* was Johnny Casino!"

Pat Birch was amazingly organized and in control during that difficult shoot. As she tells it,

"I remember putting together that dance-off. It took us a full week to shoot it. It was really the beginning of my love for doing film, because Randal graciously sort of stepped aside and let me take over. We didn't have a storyboard, but we knew where and what the action would be. We did the whole thing in a master shot first. People would be walking past each other, one couple would be talking, and another couple dancing, the next couple would be talking, and so on. Every movement was carefully blocked.

"Bill Butler, our director of photography, was great. And he used to say, 'Look, you haven't done that much film yet,' and I said, 'Yes,' and he said, 'I'm looking where you're looking because that's obviously the most important thing, and that's what we need to focus on.' And he really taught me about getting out of the scene and working through him, through what the camera sees.

"I really learned so much from him and from John Burnett, who edited the dances so terrifically. I laid out every shot in advance with John. I used to sit there with him editing that stuff, and marvel at what he could do. There's a trick shot that I don't know if anybody will ever notice, but it's in the 'hand jive' section. If you look at it very carefully, it's when Annette and John do a big turn and come down front and go around the back and then repeat the big turn coming down front again. I was in trouble there and needed a transition, so we took the same piece of film and used it twice, and no one ever caught it. John was a great editor to learn how to cut dance from."

We began filming the dance-off on July 12, at Huntington Park High School in downtown Los Angeles. It was an old school and did not have air-conditioning. What made it even worse was that Huntington Park High was around the corner from a pork plant, so there was a constant stream of stinky bacon fumes wafting in through the windows. John Travolta said, "The dance was so exciting to watch, but it was ultimately the toughest set piece in the whole movie."

The amazing Pat Birch.

Getting ready . . .

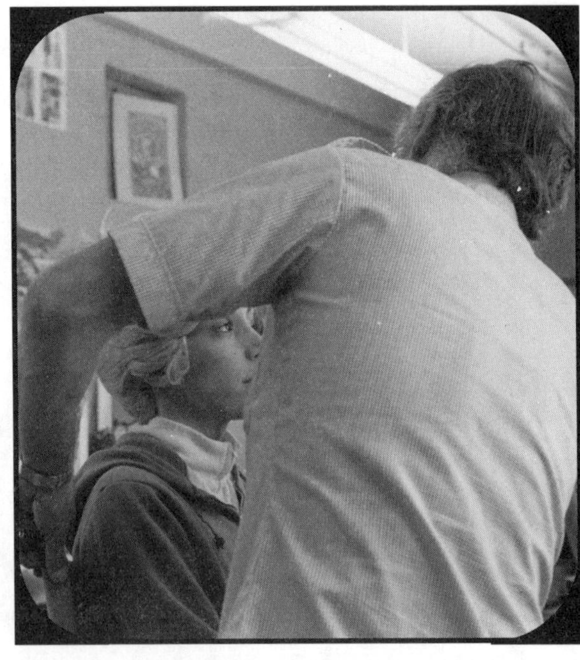

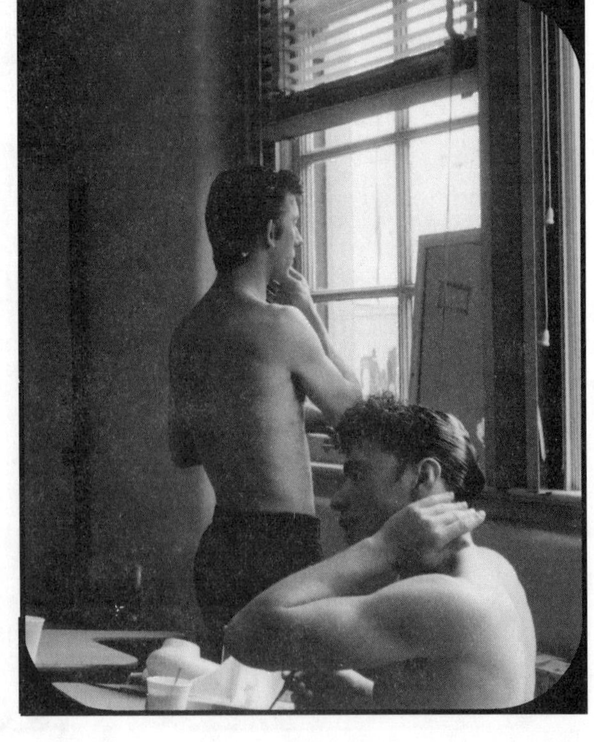

Waiting . . .

Waiting . . . and waiting in a building with no air-conditioning and pork fumes wafting in through the windows!

In between takes at the dance contest. (Center) Me and my younger brother Andrew Bernstein.

Kids all over the world know how to do the "hand jive." I wondered if it was Pat's invention.

"There already was a dance called the 'hand jive,' so I didn't invent it totally. What I added was the jumping and all the feet. I just took the pattern and enlarged on it. I took the hand jive theme and made it my own. I made a script for the whole number. Originally, all I had been told was that Danny won the contest. I think it was my idea to get Kathi Moss, who played Cha Cha on the stage, to win it with him. Kathi was a big girl, and she was a very fine Cha Cha. But she wasn't the kind of sexpot that Annette was in the movie."

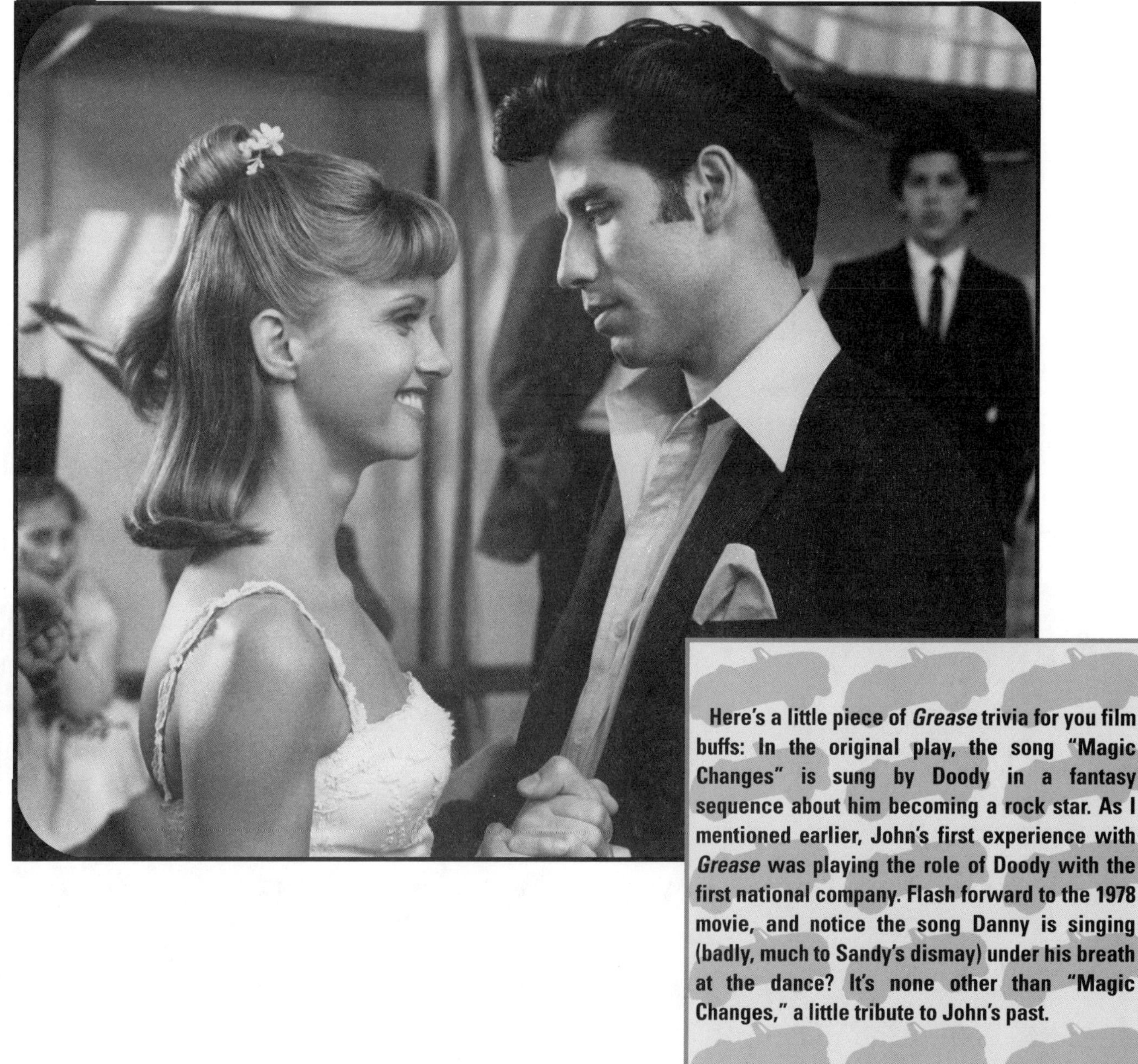

Here's a little piece of *Grease* trivia for you film buffs: In the original play, the song "Magic Changes" is sung by Doody in a fantasy sequence about him becoming a rock star. As I mentioned earlier, John's first experience with *Grease* was playing the role of Doody with the first national company. Flash forward to the 1978 movie, and notice the song Danny is singing (badly, much to Sandy's dismay) under his breath at the dance? It's none other than "Magic Changes," a little tribute to John's past.

Annette Cardona is one of the most passionate women I have ever met. I become so energized in her presence. Annette loved creating the role of Cha Cha, and she told me,

> "When the creators of *Grease* decided they wanted me to play Cha Cha, they rewrote that part. The boys made fun of Cha Cha in the stage version. So they changed that whole role around, and since then, in the Broadway show, Cha Cha is played like she is in the film. Now there is a new production of *Grease* on Broadway, and Cha Cha is played the way I created her. They incorporated the infamous dress with ruffles, too!"

I checked my script, and when Frenchy and Doody enter the gym for the dance contest, they don't have any lines. I asked Barry about that: "Well, I just looked at you and what you looked like was a beautiful, blonde pineapple. So I said it, and they kept it in."

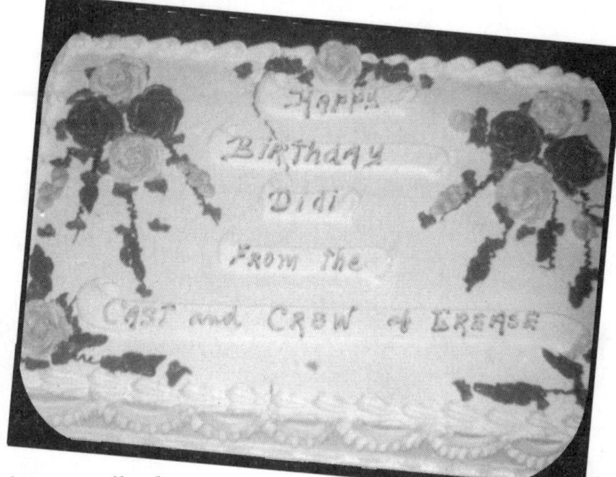

"Do you remember how hot it was in that gym?" added Barry. "Michael Tucci passed out. He had heat exhaustion and had to be taken to the hospital. He thought he was having a heart attack. It was heat prostration and the smell of the pork. I also remember you had a birthday while we were shooting that scene, and they gave you a huge, delicious cake!"

Annette and John—smokin'! (opposite page). Stockard & Dennis and Jeff & Annette dirty dancing way ahead of its time, (right and below).

I told Pat that people think the 'hand jive' sequence in the film is sped up, because it looks like we're dancing so fast. She agreed. "I remember conducting you all for sound. We really were going at high speed. Remember we had to do all the clap, clap, claps without the cameras rolling just for the sound department to have a clear sound take."

I think every cast member would agree with John Travolta when he said, "I loved that number, but if we were to measure the pain ratio, shooting that dance-off was the most painful and 'Summer Nights' was second."

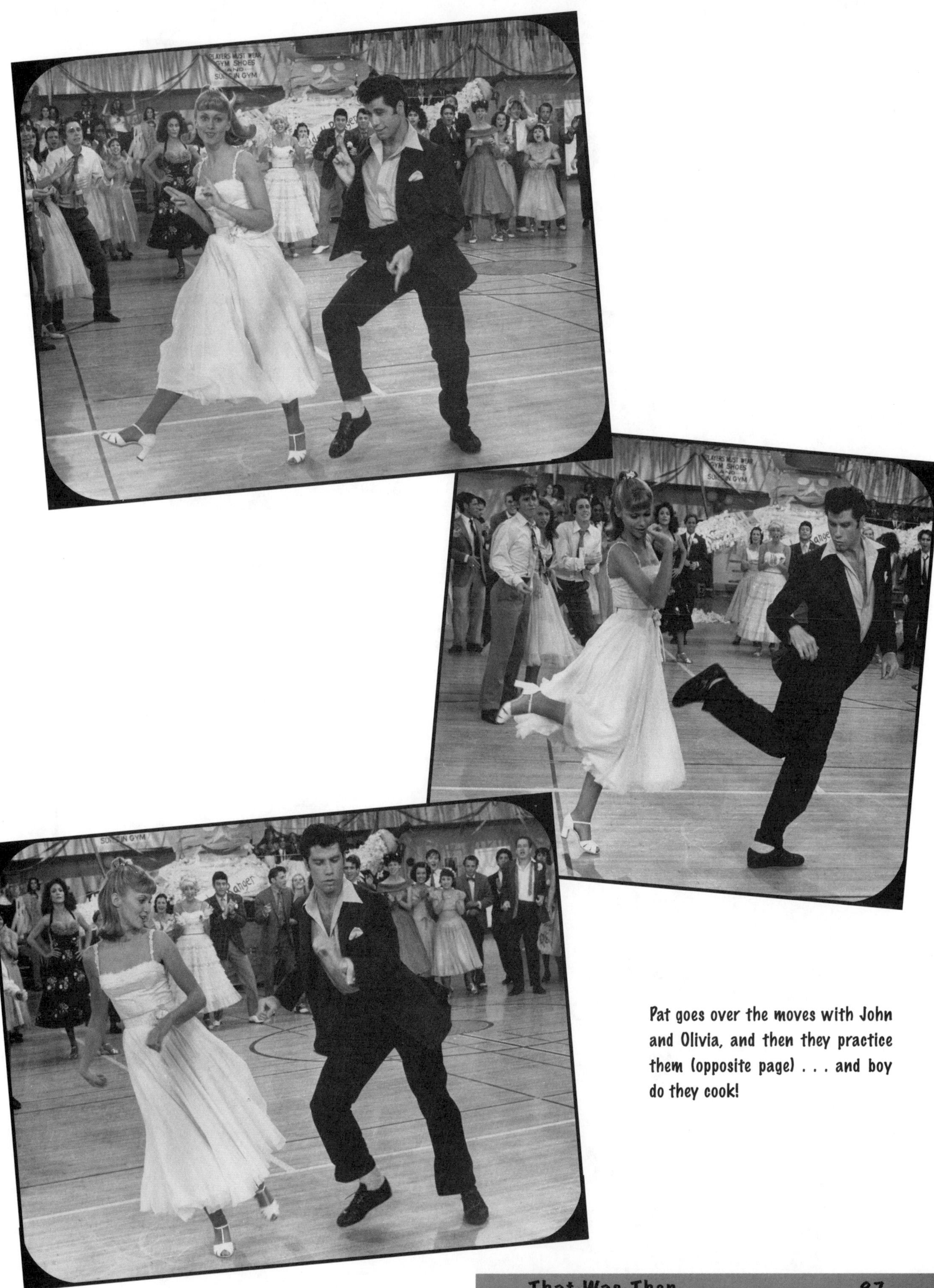

Pat goes over the moves with John and Olivia, and then they practice them (opposite page) . . . and boy do they cook!

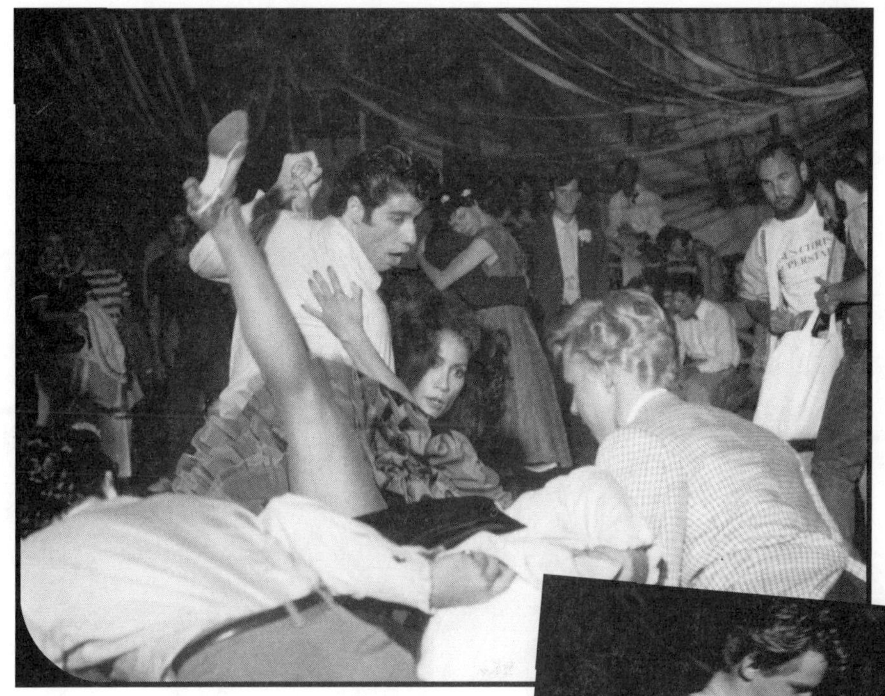

(Left) John and Annette rehearse. (Below) Wait a minute . . . could this be . . . satellite photo evidence?! Maybe not from the FBI, but evidence nonetheless that those weren't stunt butts!

(Opposite page) Eve gets more of Sid's arm than she'd prefer in a fight scene that was cut from the final version—that's Sean and Dennis duking it out. Michael spikes the punch, much to everyone's delight!

Olivia and Randal.

"Born to hand jive, oh yeah!"

Filming at the Drive-in

When we were filming a scene like the drive-in that took place at night, we would be called to the set at around 5:00 P.M. for makeup and hair, and then we would rehearse until it was dark. There were several of these night shoots on *Grease* where we worked until dawn. When you weren't needed in a shot you could take a break and rest in your trailer. Now remember, we were all playing horny teenagers and there were no "parents" around, so no one had any interest in resting. It was summertime and love was in the air.

Susan Buckner remembers these "rest" periods as a time when "Jeff and I practiced privately that scene in the dance where he pulled up my dress—tee hee." All the dressing rooms were attached to each other on one long trailer. Susan added, "There was a lot of motion in those dressing rooms—and I don't think it was earthquakes!"

Eddie Deezen had a somewhat different perspective: "I was a virgin at the time of the *Grease* shoot. I remember the guys were going to arrange for a hooker to come to my trailer and help me lose my virginity! I was terrified!! Luckily, nothing ever came of it. I was just a scared kid!"

Of course, this was all in the service of our art—we were only doing all we could to stay in character. (Tee hee, tee hee!)

Sandy

"Sandy" was another song that was written especially for the movie. Louis St. Louis, the musical director and arranger of the vocal and dance music for the original stage version of *Grease*, was brought out to Hollywood by Pat Birch and Allan Carr to do the dance arrangements for the film. But his role on the production staff kept steadily expanding. Before long, due to some dissatisfaction with the original musical director, he was asked to take over that position. And then fate truly smiled on Louis. As he remembers it,

"It was only a couple of weeks away from when John was going to have to film the drive-in sequence. We were all sitting in John's trailer—Pat, Allan, John, and me. John was saying, 'Olivia's got all these wonderful new songs,' and he wasn't belligerent about it. But he said, 'I am not singing "Alone At a Drive-in Movie." 'I want a new song for that scene.'

"And a lightbulb went off in my head, and I said, 'How stupid! What's a signature of the period?—girls' names songs.' And then I remembered that my first girlfriend's name was Sandy. I said, 'That's what you should have, a song called "Sandy"' and I remember saying that it should be a song like 'Sherry Baby' or 'Gloria' or 'Hey, Paula.' Suddenly I was going down this catalogue of girls' names songs. And then Allan said, 'Well, its three o'clock, and you're through for the day, so why don't you go home and write it?' And I said, 'I think I will.'

"I wrote the verse in the car—'Stranded at the drive-in, branded a fool/ What will they say Monday at school?' And I turned my tape recorder on, and I sang into it as I was driving down Sunset Boulevard. When I got back to the Sunset Marquis Hotel, I sat down at the piano and wrote it in twenty minutes. I called Scott Simon over to help me finish the lyrics. The Harlots—the originals, Charlett, Ola, and Sharon—were in the suite above me, and they came out on the balcony and said, 'What is that? That's gorgeous.'

"I made a little demo of 'Sandy' on a little tape recorder, took it to Allan at seven-thirty the next morning, and played it for him over breakfast. I played it for (music supervisor) Bill Oaks at eleven A.M. They played it for Stigwood, over the phone, at one P.M. They played it for John at two P.M. And at four o'clock *it was my song they were going to use in the movie*! I stayed up the whole night while they were filming John singing it. They didn't finish until seven in the morning. I knew how expensive that shoot was, and I said to myself, Once this is in the can, they're not going to change *this*. And now it's *history*!"

It wasn't all work and no play while we were making *Grease.* One Saturday the cast of *The Bad News Bears* challenged the cast of *Grease* to a softball game. Allan Carr agreed to umpire and John Travolta to pitch. The score was 4-4 when Allan called the game due to fading light. (I think that's Dinah on base, and the cast of *The Bad News Bears* in the field.)

There Are Worse Things I Could Do

During the making of *Grease*, all of the actors stayed in character all day, even when the cameras weren't rolling. We called each other by our characters' names, and we related to each other as our characters would have. Okay, here's a little secret: most of us were *more* than "a little" older than the high school kids we were playing, so staying in character gave us license to act as wild or as crazy or as *young* as we wanted to.

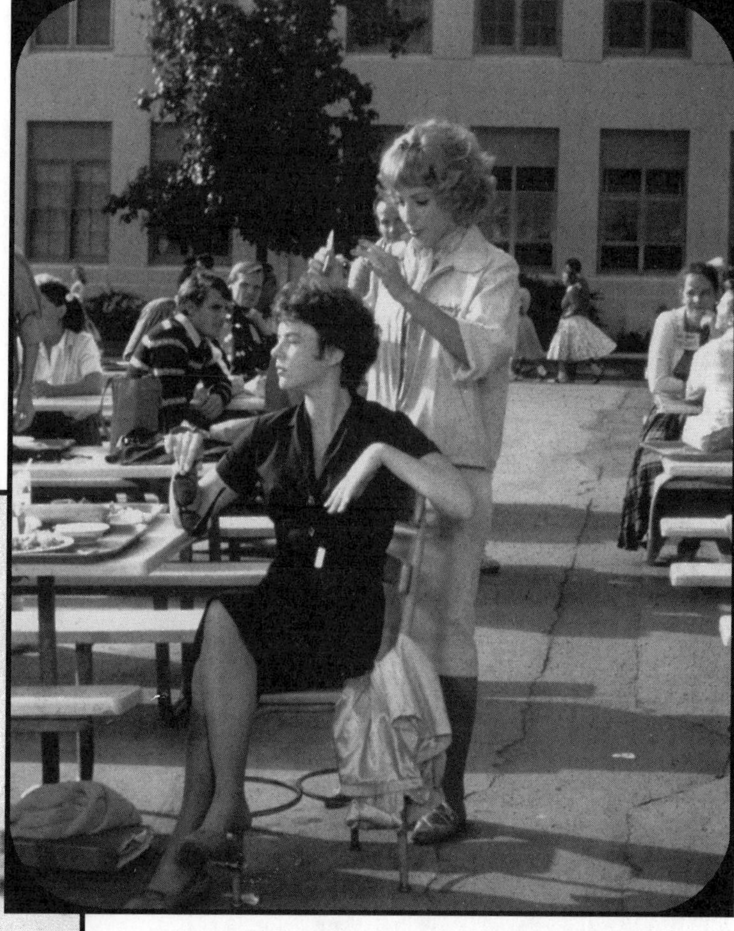

I was very moved by Rizzo's song, "There Are Worse Things I Could Do." It's her statement about who she really is. Rizzo is not a tease. She is someone who is very honest about her feelings, even if she does work hard to cover up her vulnerable side.

Stockard agrees and says, "Allan never liked that song. Pat Birch and I really campaigned, and Allan finally said he would shoot it. It felt like he was just going to shoot it and then cut it. I felt very strongly about that song, I really loved it. When they put the movie together and it stayed in, I was amazed and so happy. Allan hated it because he felt it was a downer. But I begged and pleaded, and once he shot it, I guess they liked it. I remember, too, that Jeff was really sweet because he wanted to be in the background working on his car. He insisted on being there."

THUNDER ROAD

Kenickie was way too cool ever to come right out and say how worried he was about the race at Thunder Road. Jeff Conaway was endearing and gorgeous as Kenickie. His imagination knew no bounds. He deftly captured Kenickie's vulnerability when he reached out and hugged Danny right before they left for the race. Jeff explains,

"Here's how it happened. The weekend before we were scheduled to shoot that scene I said to myself, How is this scene going to work? What could be really *special* about it? I started going over it and thinking about my relationship with Zuko, and I thought, Wouldn't it be great to see these two guys hug. But then what would happen? We would have to pretend like it didn't happen. So I called John up—we were living in the same building, you remember, down on South Doheny—and I said, 'Let me come up, I got an idea for the scene.' I went up and we rehearsed it, and the next day we went to do it, and we told Randal that we got this idea and we did it. And Randal said, 'Hey, really good, John.' But John said, 'It wasn't my idea, it was Jeff's idea.'"

I asked Randal what scene was the most difficult for him to direct. "I think probably the big chase at Thunder Road. I had never done anything like that. But it was exciting, and I had a great time doing it. I think it turned out okay."

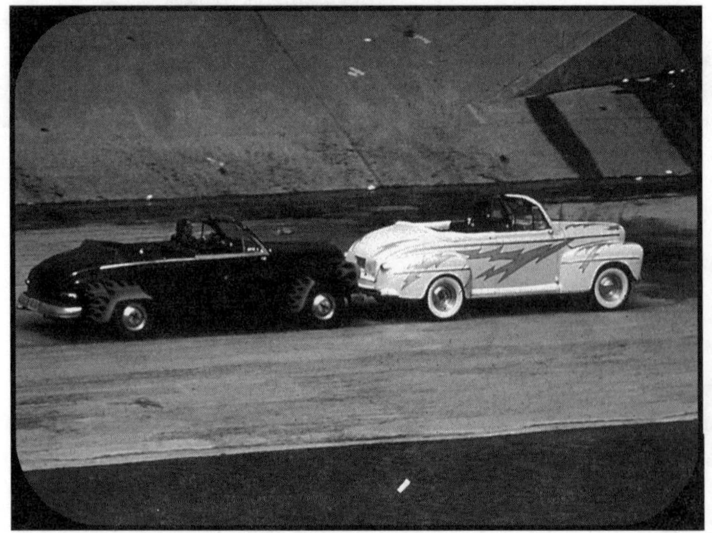

The Pink Ladies and the T-Birds were very serious in this scene. We hated the Scorpions and we wanted to beat them, but we were also afraid of them. And although few of us knew it while we were filming the scene, Annette, who looks so tough and indestructible leaning on the Scorpion's car, "Hell's Chariot," was actually in a great deal of pain.

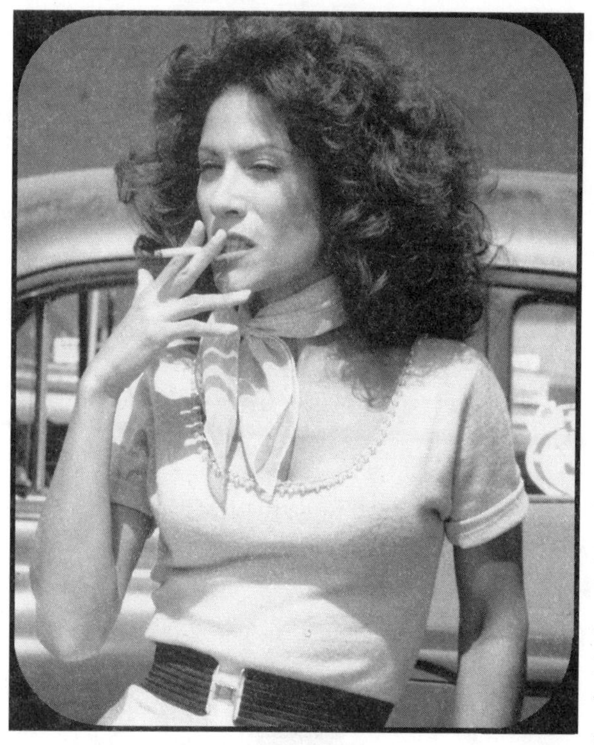

As Annette recalls, "I was in the hospital for tests the whole weekend before we filmed. Allan Carr called me there and told me not to worry about anything, he just wouldn't use me in the scene. I said, 'No way,' and he said, 'But how are you going to—' and I said, 'I don't know, but no way—I'll be there Monday morning!'

"When I told my doctor I was going to check out and do the scene, he thought I was nuts, but he had taken care of a lot of show people, so he said, 'You have got to get here right after you finish shooting and I will have the hospital waiting.' I was doubled over with pain when I shot that scene. I could hardly put those tight pants and high heels on. Did you ever notice how I was leaning on Leo's car instead of standing up? I was in so much pain they had to drive me to the actual spot where I started the race. It turned out I had a tubular pregnancy, and that night, actually, I went into surgery. I don't know how I got through that day. I really wanted to be in that scene, and I guess the lesson was, if you really want something and you set out to do it with all your heart, then your mind is capable and powerful enough to overcome any obstacles."

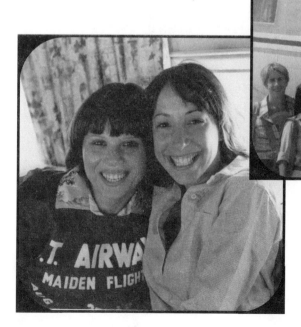

While Annette was spending her weekend in the hospital having tests, John flew a few of us to Las Vegas to see Olivia perform. It was the first time I ever went on such a small aircraft and wondered what kind of plane it was. "It was a Douglas DC-3," John tells me. "And it was old by the time I bought it, but I like antique airplanes. Basically, it was an antique airliner. I was excited about owning it and using it and about everybody coming with me to see Olivia. That was before we finished filming the movie. It was August 1977, and she had a commitment to fulfill for a gig. She was the headliner, and Kenny Rogers opened for her. That, of course, was before Kenny Rogers was Kenny Rogers. My sister Ellen came, too. I think it was Andy, Lou, Allan's assistant Linda, and you. I remember us all in our red T-shirts with the white lettering. It was a pretty neat day."

(Below) Linda Zimmerman (Allan Carr's assistant) and me on board J. T. Airways.

You're the One That I Want

At the end of "Thunder Road," Sandy decides to "say good-bye to Sandra Dee" and asks Frenchy if she could help her change her "look." And off they go to create the "new" Sandy.

Olivia really looked forward to her transformation. Her pop star image was as pure as Sandy's at that time, and the red hot mama in her was dying to make a splashy entrance into the world. This was her golden opportunity. Here's how Olivia explains it:

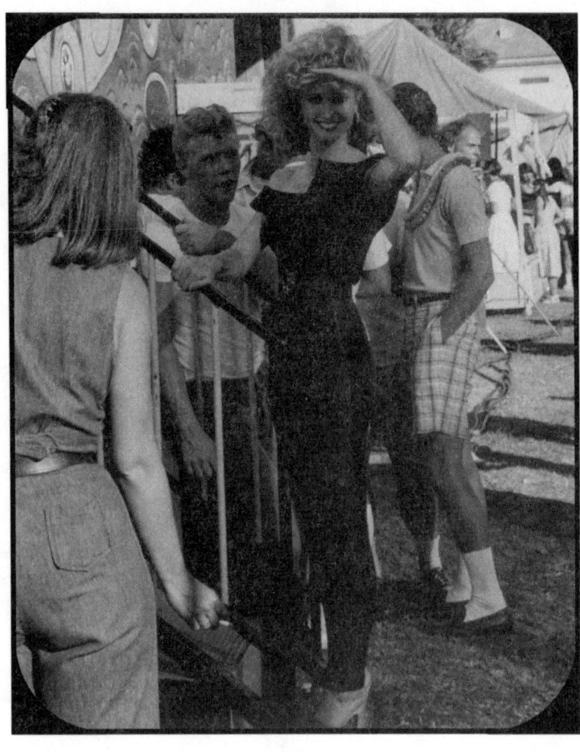

> "Sandy definitely had a 'goody-goody' image and so did I to some extent, so it was really fun for me to play a naughty girl, a character that was somewhat sexier. I think even if I wanted to, I just couldn't abruptly change from one image to another. *Grease* gave me an opportunity to make a transition to playing a little bit older and to create a little harder image which was fine, and it opened up a whole new musical thing, too. It was incredible. So doing *Grease* really was wonderful for me. I remember when I read the script I loved that I'd get the chance to be those two people. We all have little bits of both in us. That was kind of exciting."

I wondered how much input Olivia had in creating the "new" Sandy. Olivia told me,

> "Well, we went through clothes with designer Albert Wolsky. We talked about wearing black and tights, and he just brought stuff from wardrobe. I think those black pants were actually from the fifties. They were really old. Yeah, I think black was my idea. My hairdresser and I worked on my hair design, and I said, 'Do what you think would work best for the time period.' I remember that the night before shooting the carnival scene we did a practice run with the clothes. We tried on different things. The red shoes were mine. We were on location finishing up the drive-in scene. I got all dressed up and walked onto the set. I had been working with that same crew for, what was it, two months, and they didn't know it was me. I had the best time—flirting with everyone!! I thought, Here's this bad girl who gets such a different reaction—this is *fun*."

No one could get over how fantastic Olivia looked. She didn't just *look* cool on the outside—she *felt* cool on the inside. She wowed everyone—well, almost everyone.

Danny Zuko turning jock? (above). The boys rehearse "bowing down" to the new Sandra Dee (right).

His "chills are multiplying!" (above).

Dinah had a funny reaction: "I was jealous, of course. I mean, it was one thing when she was Miss Goody Two Shoes, ya know, but when she transformed—well, it just wasn't fair. I mean, that was Pink Lady territory!!"

Sean Moran's reaction summed up how all the dancers felt. "My God, we all almost died. We hadn't seen Sandy's transformation costume before. When Olivia came out, half the boys fell to their knees in amazement, and the other half wanted the outfit."

Of course I had to ask, So, Liv, did you have to diet to fit into those pants? "No, I was pretty skinny then," admits Olivia. "Luckily I didn't have to diet. I had to be stitched into those pants every morning. They didn't want to use a zipper. I don't remember what they had to do if I needed to go pee."

Allan Carr asked John Farrar to write a duet for Sandy's transformation at the end of the movie. John was thrilled and began to do some research on songs of that period. "I loved Eddie Cochran's music," he told me, "but I wanted the duet to sound like what was happening then, in the late seventies, too." John came up with the title, 'You're the One That I Want,' and he was off and running!

When he went to the carnival location to watch the filming of his song, John felt strangely confident. "John and Olivia were so great, and I remember feeling really certain for the first time in my life that we had a hit on our hands!" Even so, John Farrar is constantly surprised by the magnitude of the success of his two songs in *Grease*.

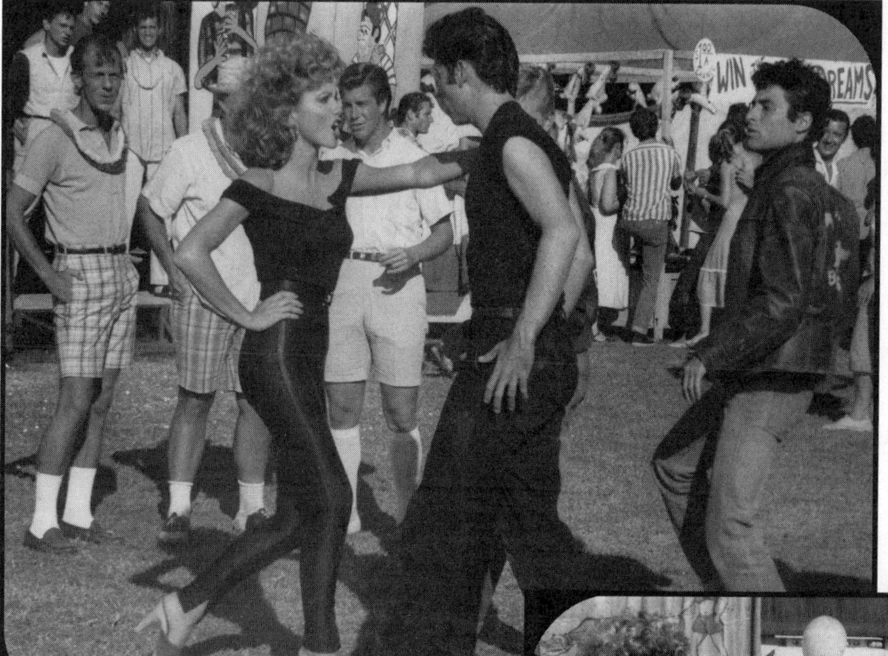

"Tell me about it, stud!"

"I better shape up!"

John "feels his way" up the ramp to the shake shack (opposite page).

SALOON

We Go Together

I loved watching Stockard work. She was so strong and fearless as Rizzo, definitely our leader. I wish I could have had her strength when I was in high school. I had a bad reputation and I didn't even *do* anything—at least not like Rizzo. I think we both just had the hots for boys. One of the few times we were alone together in a scene was at the end of the movie on the Ferris wheel. Kenickie yells up to Rizzo that he wants to make up, and Rizzo explodes with her good news. Stockard told me, describing that moment, "I saw Rizzo as very tough and defensive. The only time you ever saw the kid in her was at the end at the carnival when she found out she wasn't pregnant."

We all learn some important lessons in our senior year at Rydell. Frenchy listens to her guardian angel and goes back to high school. Danny and Sandy learn how to turn each other on. Rizzo and Kenickie stopped fighting long enough to see how crazy they are for each other. Here's how Jamie Donnelly reflected on Jan's senior year at Rydell:

I love this one of me and Stockard; Riz is smiling at last.

Jeff and Stockard rehearse with Randal the "I'm not pregnant!!" scene.

Jan all grown up by the end of the school year.

"Her relationship with the Pink Ladies made her feel stronger and helped her to really grow up that senior year. Then, having Putzie—who was such a darling boy—like her, she became more confident and began losing weight. I worked it out with our costume designer, Albert, so the audience would actually see Jan losing weight during the course of the movie. In the beginning of the movie, I am wearing very baggy clothes. By the end, you can see I'm pretty trimmed down. I'm wearing a tight green dress at the carnival. I wanted to have that progression so that through Jan's relationship with her girlfriends and then from the confidence she gains from having a little boyfriend of her own, she would have a sense of herself as an individual and be ready to go off into the world."

Kelly Ward, who played Jan's angel-faced boyfriend Putzie, loved working with Jamie.

"I was a fan of hers before I ever met her. I saw her on Broadway in a production called *Rogers & Hart,* a musical revue based on the music of the songwriting team. And she was this pixie who did incredible special material and lit up the stage. All I could think was, 'Who is that girl?' It was really unbelievable. That was in 1975. So, 'We Go Together' had special meaning for me. It's like this kind of friendship goes on forever. We made lifelong friends, and even though we have drifted apart and gone our separate ways, it's interesting, getting back together, whether it's with you or John or Olivia or Jeff or anybody. It's like the years disappear and you're right back again in that special part of your life. We *will* always be together!"

The two sides of Randal:
In charge and in the face!

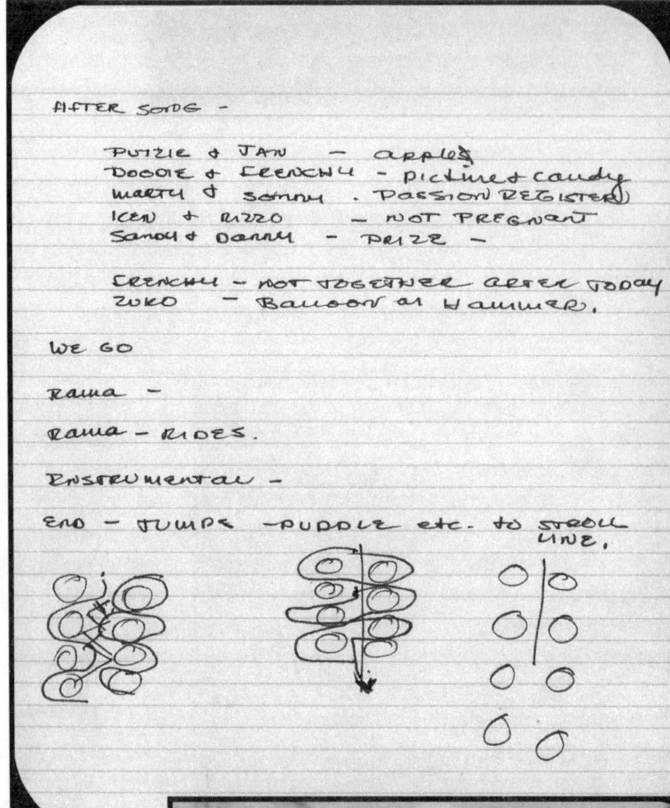

AFTER SONG -

PUTZIE & JAN - apples
DOODIE & FRENCHY - picture & candy
MARTY & SONNY - PASSION REGISTER
KEN & RIZZO - NOT PREGNANT
SANDY & DANNY - PRIZE -

FRENCHY - NOT TOGETHER AFTER TODAY
ZUKO - BALLOON at HAMMER.

WE GO

RAMA -

RAMA - RIDES.

INSTRUMENTAL -

END - JUMPS - PUDDLE etc. to STROLL LINE.

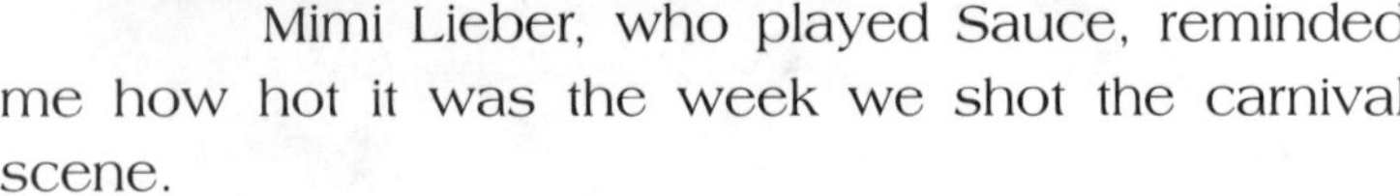

Mimi Lieber, who played Sauce, reminded me how hot it was the week we shot the carnival scene.

"When we were shooting 'We Go Together,' there was really record-breaking heat, it was 106 degrees. My sister came to visit the set one day, when we were shooting the big dance finale, the dancers' big moment! All the dancers were featured coming down the field. Then we jumped off these benches, and, you know, I was never a

Rehearsing the finale . . . and letting off some steam (top and bottom, left). Pat plans her next move (above). Pat's original blocking notes for "We Go Together" (top, right).

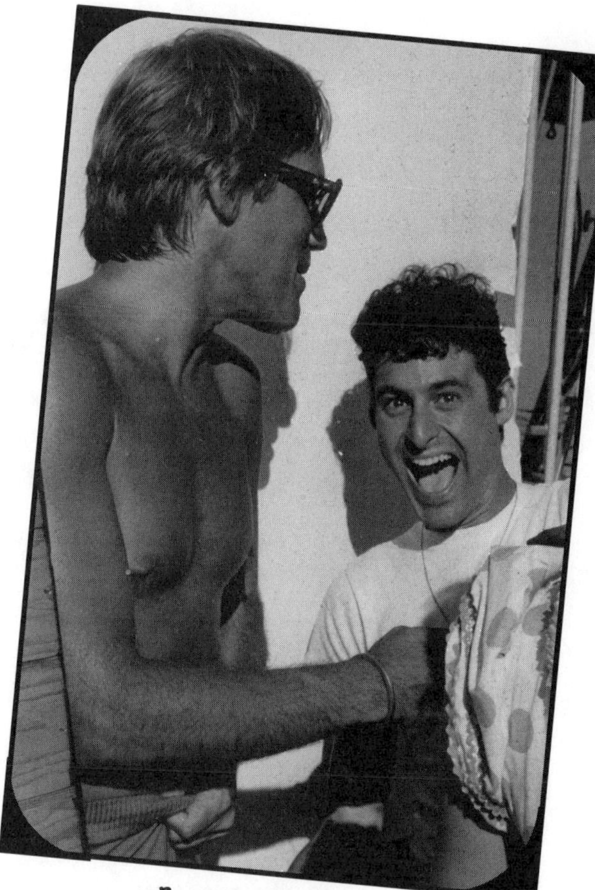

Randal and Barry.

Michael Tucci.

great jumper or leaper, but my heart and soul were in it. And I came down out of some jump and passed out from sunstroke. And all I remember is waking up, in the tent that had been set up for all of us, in John's lap—my head in John's lap and a water-soaked chamois over my face and pulling it off my face and seeing through, like a fisheye lens, everyone staring at me, first my worried sister, and then John, who was saying, 'Get back! She's not a freak in a freak show.' Imagine waking up in John Travolta's lap and not knowing how you got there?"

Boy, Mimi, I would have milked that situation for all it was worth!

• • •

Grease is about free spirits having fun, falling in love, getting into trouble, blowing off steam. It's about that wonderful, "anything can happen" part of our lives. What we performers did on the set somehow managed to capture the emotional essence of all that. Our performances were honest and truthful, and that's something we can be proud of. Our pride in our work has only deepened after twenty years, especially since we all constantly receive such positive feedback from fan after fan.

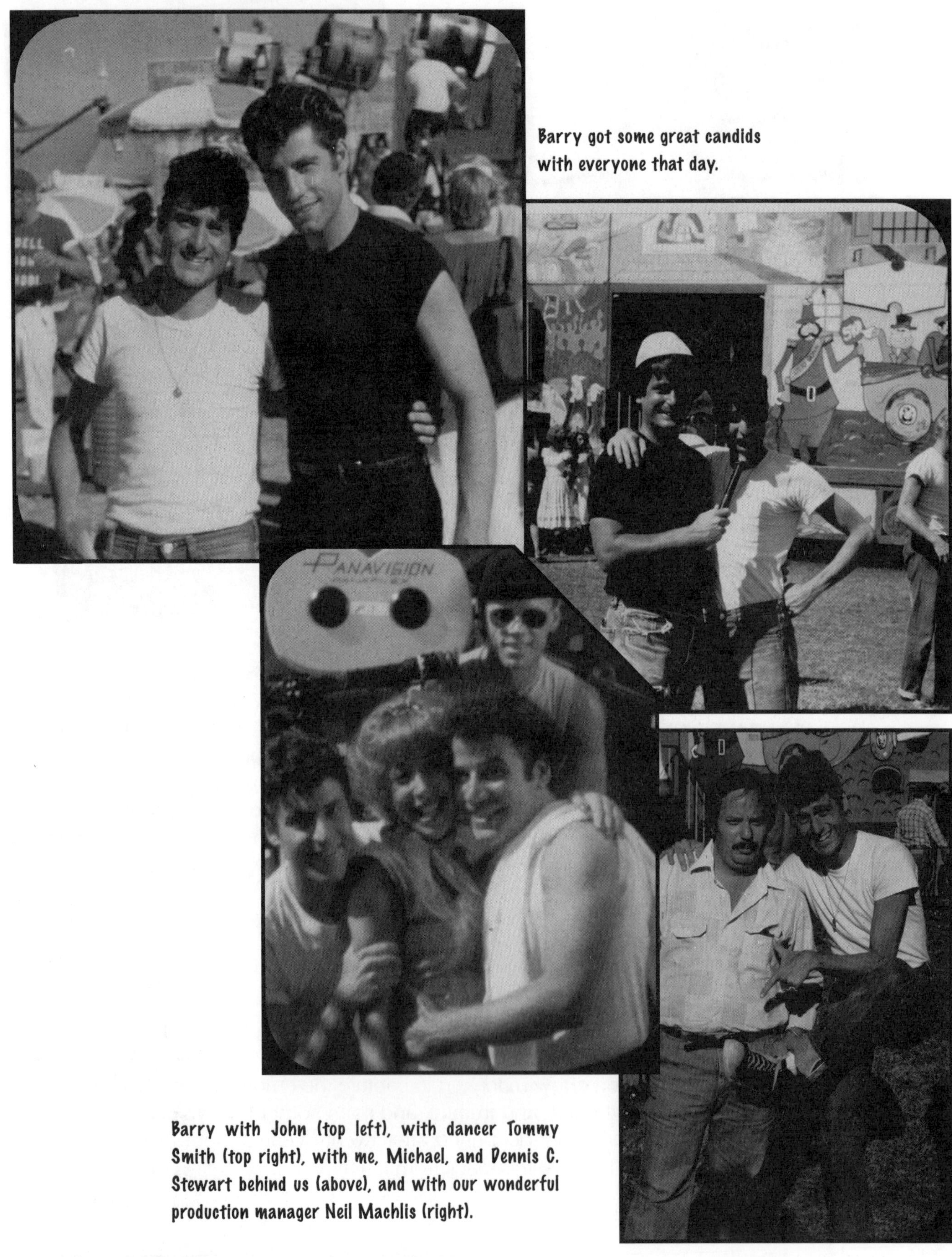

Barry got some great candids with everyone that day.

Barry with John (top left), with dancer Tommy Smith (top right), with me, Michael, and Dennis C. Stewart behind us (above), and with our wonderful production manager Neil Machlis (right).

"A wop baba lu mop . . . a wop bam boom!"

HOME
VISITORS

GYRO
CANDIED APPLES
CANDIED APPLES

"We'll always be together!"

PARTY TIME!

The Cast Party

On the last day of filming, after the last shot was completed, Randal announced to the whole cast and crew, "It's a wrap!" Everyone started crying. The cast began to applaud the crew, and the crew in turn applauded us. We had become so close, one big gang. It was definitely an emotional time. We weren't going to be spoiled anymore in our own protected, pampered world. Three months is a long time, and now the party was over.

But another one was about to begin. Our wrap party was held the next evening at Paramount. Carol Bayer Sager must have been inspired by Allan Carr's party-giving prowess when she wrote "Nobody Does It Better." He *is* the best.

My memory of that night is a little bit hazy. I remember I wanted my hair to look good because everyone had only seen me in a wig all summer. So I went and had a perm. (I guess even though the filming was over, I hadn't shed the character of Frenchy just yet.) Also, I remember telling the head of the props department, Richard Valesko, that after all my recent gum-chewing, I was afraid I really needed to go to the dentist. He told me he wasn't surprised, because the cast chewed about 100,000 pieces of bubble gum over the course of the summer, as many as five thousand pieces a day!

The music at the party was great. It was a combination of disco and bop. We danced all night and exchanged presents. John gave me a sterling silver heart from

Tiffany's with the inscription "J. T. and D. C." on the front and "*Grease,* the Movie" on the back. Stockard gave all the Pink Ladies gold whistles on long gold chains which you could wear around your neck or as a belt. (It was the seventies and gold chain belts were really big then.) The inscription, on a little gold medallion, read: "Frenchy, Love, Riz 9-13-77." Stockard was having so much fun. She was happy, giddy, exuberant. So were we all, come to think of it, thanks to another present she gave us—some irresistible brownies she made from a recipe she apparently found in *The Alice B. Toklas Cook Book.* (I guess that's why my memory is somewhat murky.) The T-Birds gave everyone a button with that picture on it of the three of them mooning. The inscription, naturally, was: "THE END—Love, Putzie, Doody and Sonny." The producers gave us beautiful Rydell jackets, and we celebrated until dawn.

Grease Publicity Tour

Around the third week in May 1978, I was sent out on a nationwide publicity tour. I hadn't even seen the movie yet, only a film clip of "Beauty School Dropout," which Paramount gave me to use on the tour. I went to about a dozen cities in five days for interviews with local papers and appearances on television and radio talk shows.

I'll never forget one interview I had on a live radio talk show in Detroit. The disc jockey said, "I see here in your bio that your first job in Hollywood was working with Henry Winkler. Now that you've worked with John Travolta as well, what would you say is the main difference between the two of them?" And I innocently responded, "Oh, about three inches!" Well, the dee-jay's earphones almost popped off his head, and I quickly added, "Their *height,* of course!"

A ROBERT STIGWOOD/ALLAN CARR PRODUCTION

GREASE

AMERICA'S FAVORITE ROCK 'N' ROLL NEW '50'S MUSICAL

Robert Stigwood and Allan Carr are pleased to invite you and a guest to a very special preview screening of:

GREASE

Thursday, June 1, 1978

8:30 PM

SAMUEL GOLDWYN THEATRE

Academy of Motion Picture Arts and Sciences

8949 Wilshire Boulevard

Beverly Hills, California

PLEASE NOTE: NO ONE WILL BE ADMITTED UNLESS THEIR NAME APPEARS ON THE DOOR LIST. PLEASE R.S.V.P. TO: 463-0100, Ext. 1476.

Paramount Pictures Corporation

5451 Marathon Street, Los Angeles, California 90038 (213) 463-0100

GW LEISURE TIME GRO

GREASE

GREASE PROM
9665 Wilshire Boulevard, Suite 200
Beverly Hills, California 90212

Att: Dale Olson

GREASE
R.S.V.P.
Name Didi Conn (please print)
will attend ☑
will not attend ☐
the Premiere and Prom Party
Sunday, June 4, 1978

GREASE PROM
9665 Wilshire Boulevard, Suite 200
Beverly Hills, California 90212
Att: Dale Olson Phone: 275-9145/275-1453

The First Look

On June 1, the cast and crew were given a private screening of *Grease* at the Samuel Goldwyn Theater at the Academy of Motion Picture Arts and Sciences in Beverly Hills. Almost a year had gone by since we completed filming, so we were all thrilled to see each other again. The theater was alive with nervous energy and squeals of delight, and there was lots of hugging and kissing. Everyone in my row held hands as the lights went down, and suddenly we were finally seeing the result of all our hard work.

I remember thinking how beautiful Olivia looked and how touched I was by her acting in the opening scene. Then the animated titles began, and that tube squirted out the title of the movie. We had no idea the opening titles were animated. The whole audience went berserk—we got hysterical. Everyone was cheering so loudly you couldn't hear the sound track. Then I saw the pink billboard with my name on it and just couldn't believe it. My heart was beating like crazy. You know how you feel when you go to pick up some rolls of film you took of a fantastic vacation and you can't wait to open the envelope and see how the photos turned out? Well, imagine that your photos are forty-eight feet high and eighty feet wide!

Curiously, what sticks out in my mind are some of the bloopers I caught—like how my character's name was spelled "Frenchy" in the main titles, but "Frenchie" in the closing credits. And how Joan Blondell went to turn off a light switch with her elbow because her hands were full, and she missed the switch by about six inches but it went off anyway.

By the end of the movie many of us were crying, but I have to confess, it wasn't just because we were moved to tears by how overwhelmingly good the movie was—

we really missed several big sections of scenes that were cut from the final film. When you act on the stage, you are in total control of your performance. It's between you and your local electric company—as long as the lights stay on, your work is seen. But that's not the case in films. The director and the editor can delete any part of your performance in the cutting room.

The movie went by so quickly it shocked us. I was afraid the heart of the movie had been sacrificed for its lightning-fast pace. At the end, Pat Birch looked at me and said, "Oh, look how moved Didi is!" And I thought, Yeah, I'm moved—to get out of here as fast as I can! I didn't know how to react, and I didn't know what to say. I thought I looked like an A-number-one weirdo. Who would ever hire someone who looked so outrageous? Then Marion Dougherty, the head of casting at Paramount who was sitting behind me, tapped me on the shoulder and said, "Didi, you are going to be a major, major star." Well, *that* kinda perked me up—the woman who oversaw all of the casting at one of the major motion picture studios was now a fan of mine, and my future was beginning to look a little brighter. But whatever ambivalence I felt about my own work, there was no denying how sensational John and Olivia were and how tremendously exciting and appealing the movie was.

When we were filming *Grease, Saturday Night Fever* hadn't come out yet. Although John had been a sex symbol for years as Vinnie Barbarino in "Welcome Back Kotter," his career skyrocketed with the release of *Saturday Night Fever*. He received extraordinary critical acclaim and won the Best Actor Award from The National Society of Film Critics. Topping it off was a 1977 Academy Award nomination as Best Actor. John invited us all to a screening of *Saturday Night Fever* while we were still filming *Grease*, and we were all blown away by his performance. But he was extremely critical of his work. As hard as it is to believe, he truly didn't know how gifted and brilliant he was.

The World Premiere

On June 2, *Grease* received its world premiere before an invited audience at Mann's Chinese Theater in Hollywood. My date was Barry Pearl, and we went in a white limo with my mother, Beverly Shmerling, my Auntie Rachel Lehmann, my brothers Richard and Andrew Bernstein, and friends Jim Caswell and Abe and Kathy Rogland.

What a night! Here's how Wanda McDaniel from *The Los Angeles Herald-Examiner* described the event:

> "At the world premiere of *Grease*, Hollywood came back to town. The scene at Mann's Chinese Theater Sunday night was straight out of Tinseltown lore in its purest sense. . . .
>
> "*Grease* producer and back-to-glamour crusader Allan Carr was in his element with the film's co-star Stockard Channing, and his fellow producer Robert Stigwood brought screaming fits to the throng, thanks in part to his date, Lily Tomlin.
>
> ". . . Midway into the clamor, Mayor Tom Bradley stepped up to the microphone to proclaim this day 'Grease' Day.

World Premiere at Mann's Chinese Theatre, Hollywood, California, June 4, 1978.

Mom, me, Barry, and Auntie Rachel (top, right). Me, Barry, and Army Archerd (middle, right). Lily Tomlin and *Grease* producer Robert Stigwood (bottom, right).

"... Travolta's limo, carrying his *Grease* costar Olivia Newton-John, may never be the same. The shrieking lines of Travolta addicts had spotted his famous mug, sparking a Sunday night fever that dominoed through the crowd. They were touching his car, begging for his attention.

"Delirium had firmly set in when the two were finally able to emerge from the car for the exclusive screening. Wearing the black leather "T Bird" gang jacket and black T-shirt he wore in the movie, Travolta had emptied a bottle of hair grease for authenticating the occasion. And Olivia, in a full-skirted gown and flowers, came decked for the prom.

"... *Grease* lightning had struck Hollywood."

Allan was fond of quoting Blanche Dubois's famous line, "I don't want reality, I want the magic." He had orchestrated a perfect evening. The premiere party was held at Paramount, where over a thousand people crowded onto a soundstage which had been masterfully decorated to look just like a high school prom. Olivia changed into a skin-tight shocking pink jumpsuit and looked sensational.

And once again we danced all night!

Lorenzo Lamas kissing my Auntie Rachel (above, left). My mom, Beverly, and Olivia's mom, Irene (above). Me and Andy Tennant dancing (left).

Jamie Donnelly ("Jan"), me ("Frenchy"), and Pat Birch (top left), and Olivia, my mom, John, and Stockard (top right). Times Square, June 13, 1978 (above). New York Premiere Party Invitation at Loew State 1 (right).

John Travolta
Olivia Newton-John
GREASE
TM
ADMIT ONE
Date: Tuesday, June 13th
Time: 8:00 PM

Olivia Newton-John (left). Olivia and her mom, Irene Newton-John (below).

Me and my beautiful mom (above). Michael Eisner, John Travolta, and Auntie Rachel Lehmann (right).

Next the party moved east to the Big Apple. *Grease* opened in New York on Tuesday night, June 13, 1978, at the Loews State 1 Theater on Broadway and 45th Street.

Here's how George Christy of *The Hollywood Reporter* described the premiere party at Studio 54:

> ". . . Studio 54 in New York is really another country, where host Steve Rubell is King. Tuesday, a cast of thousands, including Liza (Minelli) and Elizabeth (Taylor) poured into the polished-parquet palace to applaud Allan Carr and Robert Stigwood. 'Steve Rubell has *never* decorated Studio 54 like this,' offered (Head of Publicity) Larry Mark, who masterminded the night-long premiere party, where open-topped roadsters and hot dog stands conveyed the fifties mood. 'Steve's done this because he loves Allan.'"

The New York reviews were terrific. Vincent Canby of *The New York Times* gave *Grease* a rave:

> "*Grease* is a contemporary fantasy about a 1950s musical—a larger, funnier, wittier, and more imaginative-than-Hollywood movie with a life that is all its own . . . The movie is also terrific fun . . . The gang at old Rydell High is loaded with the kind of talent and exuberance you don't often find very far from a musical stage . . . *Grease* is the best movie musical we've had in years . . . Its sensibility is not tied to the past

Conn's earning a place in the spotlight

By LAURA de VINCENT

In Paramount Pictures' new 1950s musical "Grease," actress Didi Conn flunks out of beauty school, has a visitation from Teen Angel Frankie Avalon and hangs out at the malt shop, a teen-age training ground for the singles bars of the '70s.

In real life back in 1956, Didi Conn wore pedal pushers and watched "Howdy Doody," "Fury," "Topper" and "My Little Margie."

"But my most vivid recollections of Brooklyn in the mid-'50s are of my brother doing the lindy with my aunt," Conn said during a recent stop in New Orleans to promote "Grease." "He wouldn't dance with me to 'Rock Around the Clock,' so most of the time I collected insects — ants and lightning bugs and other creatures I didn't especially like — with a boy in the neighborhood I played with.

"I must have liked the guy very much. But I stopped playing with him when he ate a caterpillar."

CONN PLAYS Frenchy, a scatterbrained, aspiring beautician, in "Grease" following a part in the TV movie "Murder at the Mardi Gras" and the lead in last year's hit "You Light Up My Life."

But although she can still walk through a hotel lobby without being pounced on by fans, some day John Travolta may be asked during an interview what it's like to work with Didi Conn. She has a determination about acting quite unlike the lightheaded Frenchy of "Grease," and she is not discouraged by the fact it was Debbie Boone who made the theme song from her movie too familiar.

Conn has decided to turn down television roles in order to develop stronger characterizations, which she feels she must do "to earn my right to be in front of a camera." Although she has only a small part in "Grease," she researched her character and the period, going to screenings of "Rebel Without a Cause" and "Let the Good Times Roll" and reading all the magazines from the '50s she could find in the library.

"For our auditions, we had to dress up as our concept of the character, so I went to the beauty parlor and had my hair done up elaborately," she said. "On my way to dancing class one day, I saw a place named Frenchy's Beauty Parlor, so I went in and spent the afternoon with Frenchy, figuring she would have known someone like my character in 'Grease' when she was in beauty school. I learned from Frenchy there are a lot of psychology classes in beauty school — even one on how to get your client to like you." She even sat in on beauty college classes.

CONN RECALLS feeling like "a goof ball" every time she had to put on her character wig, but she was able to identify with some of Frenchy's traits. "I have Frenchy's drive and her good sense of humor. Her vistas are a little more compact than mine and her frame of reference is smaller, but that's because she's younger and 98 per cent of her life involves her

family. B[...] dream ab[...] ed about [...]

Broadw[...] but she h[...] cently be[...] two film[...] Frenchy [...] fied with [...]

"I saw [...] once wi[...] "Many m[...] movie t[...] whole r[...] Newton-J[...] was only [...]

She is [...] her appre[...] reason fo[...] bration a[...] the perio[...] much mo[...] The '50s [...] ry, and [...] memories [...]

CONN [...] substance [...] but at le[...] homewor[...]

"I was [...] explained [...] have elab[...] wore litt[...] model ca[...] Travolta [...] open the [...]

THE CONN VERSION

If there were a Gish sister of today, she could be Didi Conn. The Brooklyn-born actress certainly updates sweet tenderness, as evidenced by her vulnerability in such films as "You Light Up My Life," "Almost Summer" and "Grease." A veteran of early Seventies commercials, she's as hard-working (with TV movies and an off-Broadway revival of Ionesco's "The Lesson" keeping her busy) as she is touching. If there's an official waif for the

[...]he spares no effort in developing her roles.

[...]o use it, but [...]ood of the [...]e the '50s in [...]ects will be [...] to starring [...]equel, she'll be the lead in "Almost Summer."

"The philosophy of that film is respect for teen-age problems," s[...] "When you're a teen-ager and you [...] in the morning with a pimple and y[...] a date that night, you say you're [...] kill yourself, and you mean it."

but to a freer-wheeling, well-informed, high-spirited present. *Grease* is nothing but fun. It's pop entertainment of an extremely clever, energetic sort, sung and danced with style . . . !"

On September 13, 1978, *Grease* had its Paris premiere, and the newswire reported:

IN FRANCE WHERE *GREASE* OPENED ON THE 13TH, PICTURE TALLIED MAMMOUTH 25,554 ADMISSIONS IN 25 PARIS CINEMAS COMPARED TO 11,043 FOR *SATURDAY NIGHT FEVER* IN 23 HOUSES. THIS FOLLOWED TRIUMPHANT PREMIERE AND PARTY AT DEAUVILLE FESTIVAL LAST SATURDAY.

The next day *Grease* opened in London and this newswire followed:

GREASE PREMIERE IN LONDON AN EVENT OF RIOT PROPORTIONS. BIGGEST HAPPENING OF ITS KIND EVER ACCORDING TO POLICE, INCLUDING DAYS OF BEATLES. UNPRECEDENTED COVERAGE ON FRONT PAGE EVERY NATIONAL

The Toronto premiere.

Me and my big brother Bradley Bernstein.

TABLOID (READERSHIP OVER 11,000,000) AND ON ALL TV AND RADIO NEWS INCLUDING FILM CLIPS ON FORMER. PARTY ONE OF MOST SUCCESSFUL EVENTS EVER HELD HERE.

UK BUSINESS SEEMS CERTAIN TO BE RECORD-BREAKING PROPORTIONS. EMPIRE THEATRE IN LONDON WEST END ALREADY HAS POSTED RECORD ADVANCE TICKET SALE OF POUNDS 52,125 DOLLARS 104,250. PICTURE, OF COURSE, ALREADY OFF TO RECORD-SHATTERING START IN AUSTRALIA AND SOUTH AFRICA.

AT LONDON PREMIERE RIOT POLICE COULD NOT CONTROL MASS HYSTERIA AND BOTH STARS GOT NEARLY CRUSHED IN MELEE BUT WERE UNHURT.

Grease would be called *Brilliantino* in Italy, *Gummina* in France, and *Vaselina* in Mexico, and chalk up record grosses in those countries as well.

After sixty-six days, *Grease* grossed $101,150,000 in its national release alone. It achieved the $100 million box office milestone sooner than any motion picture in Paramount's history and became the second most successful film for the company. *The Godfather*, Paramount Pictures' top-grossing film up to that time, earned $100 million in 136 days of release. By December 18, 1978, *Grease* had grossed $132,472,560 in its domestic showings. By May 23, 1979, the film became Paramount Pictures' all-time top-grossing film, surpassing *The Godfather.*

We were a hit!

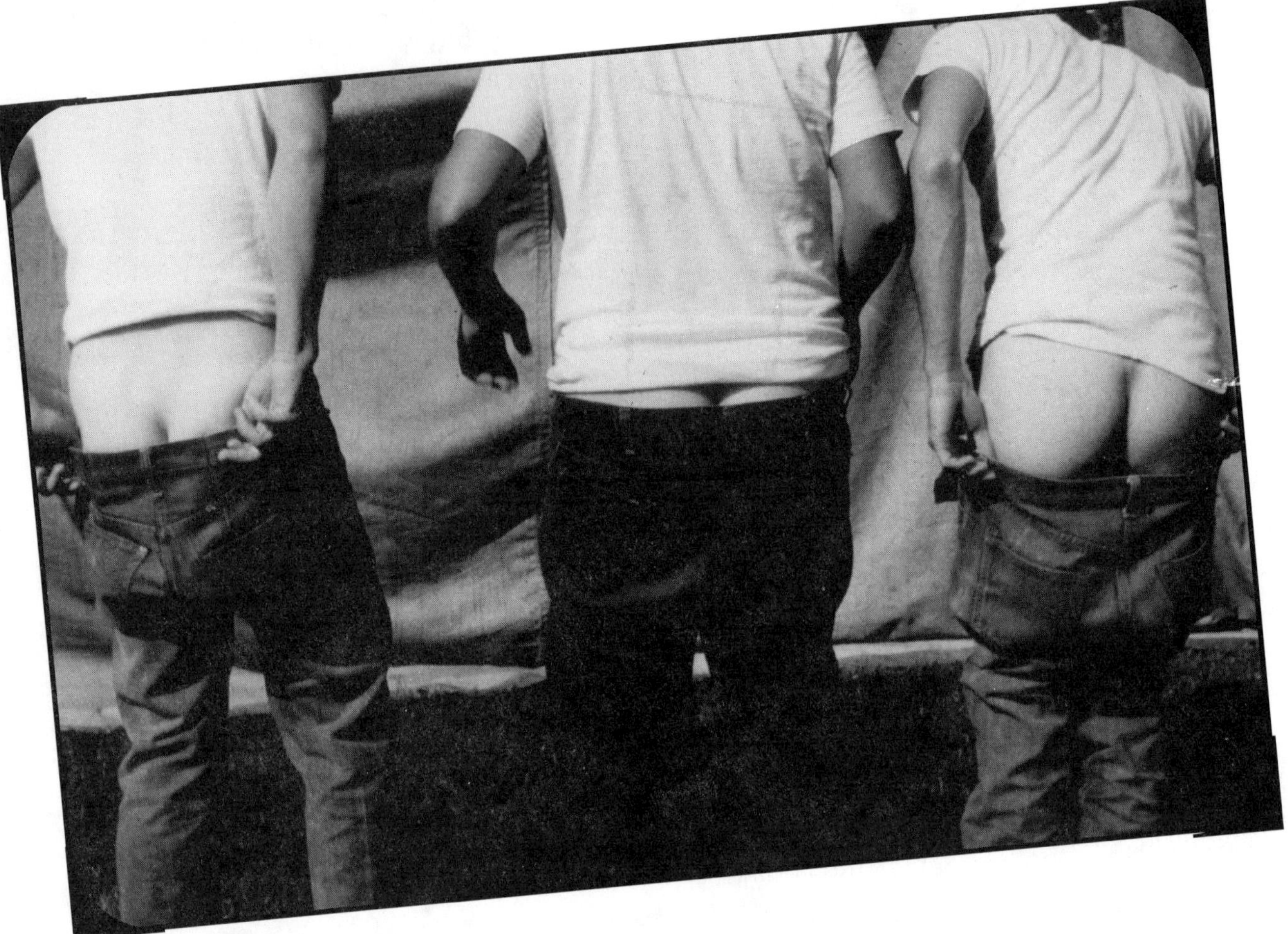

Almost the end . . .

CHAPTER 5

THIS IS NOW: Catching Up with the Cast and Crew of *Grease*

About two years ago, at around nine at night, I was happy to receive a call from Olivia because I hadn't spoken to her for a long time. She was giggling and asked if I would meet her at a restaurant in Hollywood in an hour. I said that of course I would. My stepson Matt and a few of my friends from the Broadway play *Lost in Yonkers* were visiting. We all piled into my car and off we went. Olivia was at the restaurant with Randal Kleiser and Joel Thurm. They just finished shooting a movie called *It's My Party*. After we had some nachos and orange juice, Olivia said, "Let's go!" It was all so mysterious and a lot of fun. I had no idea where we were going, but I soon found out. Right down the street was a movie theater that was playing *Grease* at a midnight screening. What a surprise, especially since I hadn't seen the movie since it opened in 1978!

We went into the theater and it was packed. When the lights went down, the audience cheered. Then came the biggest shock of all. As the movie played, the whole audience kept reciting Sandy and Danny's dialogue along with them! They sang along with all the songs, too. It was a riot! I had heard about midnight screenings of *The*

Rocky Horror Show, but I had no idea that *Grease* had a cult following, too. I must admit that the audience didn't recite *all* the dialogue, just the lines in their favorite scenes. It really cracked me up to hear everyone say in unison, "Men are rats. Worse. Fleas on rats. Worse than that. Amoebas on fleas on rats... The only man a girl can depend on is her daddy." Word must have gotten around that we were in the audience, because when we left the theater, the whole audience was waiting for us outside, and when they saw us they cheered! It was a young crowd, and everyone was so happy to see us that it made Olivia and me cry.

Twenty years is a long time. It's a whole generation. Young people who are now discovering *Grease* for the first time are the *children* of the audience who saw it when it originally premiered.

I remember having an argument with Randal and Allan when they wanted Frenchy to have colored hair in the last scene of the movie at the carnival. They wanted to film a closeup of green cotton candy and then have the camera pan up to reveal Frenchy with GREEN hair! Frenchy's explanation would be that she jumped into a swimming pool with her blonde hair and the chlorine made it green. I didn't like that idea. I didn't think it was funny. It was bad enough having red, yellow and pink hair in one movie—green hair was just too much. I mean, who would walk around with green hair? Well, just a few years later, punk hair became the fashion craze, and all over the world, young people were walking around with GREEN hair! So you see what can happen in a few years.

Well, it's now twenty years later, and I thought you might be interested to see some recent photos of the *Grease* family and learn where its members are today and what they have been doing. Also, I asked a number of the actors what they think their characters might have been up to over the past two decades, and I got some amusing answers.

OLIVIA NEWTON-JOHN

I've gotten together with Olivia regularly through the years, but when we last chatted she was full of especially exciting news. "I have a new album coming out in May," she said. "I've gone back to country music, my roots, and how I started in music in America. In Nashville, I met with all the record companies, and I'm just about to sign a new deal with MCA. There will be a lot of songs that I wrote on the album, too."

After *Grease*, Olivia was honored by Her Royal Highness Queen Elizabeth II and received the prestigious OBE (Order of the British Empire).

Her next album, *Totally Hot*, was a crossover and turned Olivia from a country pop singer to a pop star. The sound track for *Xanadu* was both a double platinum and Top Four LP. *Physical*, the album, video, and single, gave Olivia a new image and a big hit. In 1981, she was honored with a star on Hollywood Boulevard's famous Walk of Fame.

Olivia was reunited with John Travolta in the film, *Two of a Kind*. She starred in *A Mom for Christmas* on NBC and *A Christmas Romance* with Gregory Harrison for CBS.

In 1992, Olivia released *Back to Basics: The Essential Collection 1971–1992*, her eighteenth album. Her next album, *GAIA: One Woman's Journey*, chronicled her triumphant battle with breast cancer. The entire album was written and coproduced by Olivia, and each song examined changes in her life, values, and emotions. "I think what it's made me realize," Olivia told me, "is the value of simplicity, nature, and relationships over things, money, and possessions, because those latter things are not what make you happy."

Olivia, John Farrar, and Sir Cliff Richard.

In 1995, Olivia was the host of an Australian TV series called *Wildlife*. One of the highlights of this series was Olivia interviewing the former Russian Premier Mikhail Gorbachev while on location in Moscow.

Last February was the twenty-fifth anniversary of the United Nations Environment Programme. It chose this occasion and that of International Woman's Day to honor twenty-five contemporary women from around the world, Olivia among them, who, "through their personal efforts and achievements, serve as inspiration for all toward informed and responsible actions for the protection of the planet."

I was present at the UN to see Olivia receive her award. She told me how it felt to be so highly honored. "I was very excited to be part of that very distinguished group of women. I have been the Goodwill Ambassador for UNICEF for three years, and now I'm the spokeswoman for CHEC, the Children's Health and Environmental Coalition.

Me, Olivia, and Chloe at the United Nations.

"I also support all the breast cancer groups, the Coalition and the Breast Cancer Council. The reason I am happy to talk about my experience with breast cancer is that there are so many women who have to deal with it.

"If someone who just found out she had breast cancer asked me for advice, I would tell her to get all the most up-to-date information she could, because there are a lot of new theories out there, and more and more doctors feel that you don't have to take such radical action as used to be so often recommended. I do believe in Western medicine, but you must take care of yourself spiritually as well. Try to find some kind of prayer or meditation, something to keep yourself centered. Give yourself daily affirmations that you will be healed and that you are strong. Send white light to yourself. It's really important, because mind, body, and spirit work together.

"I have a beautiful, amazing daughter named Chloe. We have three dogs. I just lost one, my beautiful Scarlett, who got run over. But I am lucky to have Scarlett's daughter, because she had eight puppies eighteen months ago. And I have Snowy, who is nearly ten now, and a new Pomeranian puppy named Rouge. We also have two cats, two birds, goldfish, a carp in a pond outside, and two horses who are kind of retired now! That's our little menagerie."

Didi: Olivia, you recently filmed an episode of "Murphy Brown" where you played yourself. I heard the studio audience gave you a standing ovation. What was that like?
Olivia: It was amazing. I never felt so loved, and I was deeply moved. It was very emotional. I was really happy to do the show.

Didi: Liv, What do you think Sandy would be doing twenty years later?
Olivia: Oh, I think she has developed her own cosmetic line called "Sandra Dee" cosmetics and she has her own makeover studio—like you see on "Oprah." She sells her products on a home shopping network and maybe has her own talk show where she does fantastic makeovers. Also, she is a terrific hairstylist as well as a talented makeup artist.

Didi: Did Sandy marry Danny?
Olivia: She and Danny lived together in a trailer camp for several years. Then Danny joined the Air Force and was stationed abroad. I think she'll always love Danny. He was her first love. Maybe they'll meet up again sometime—who knows!

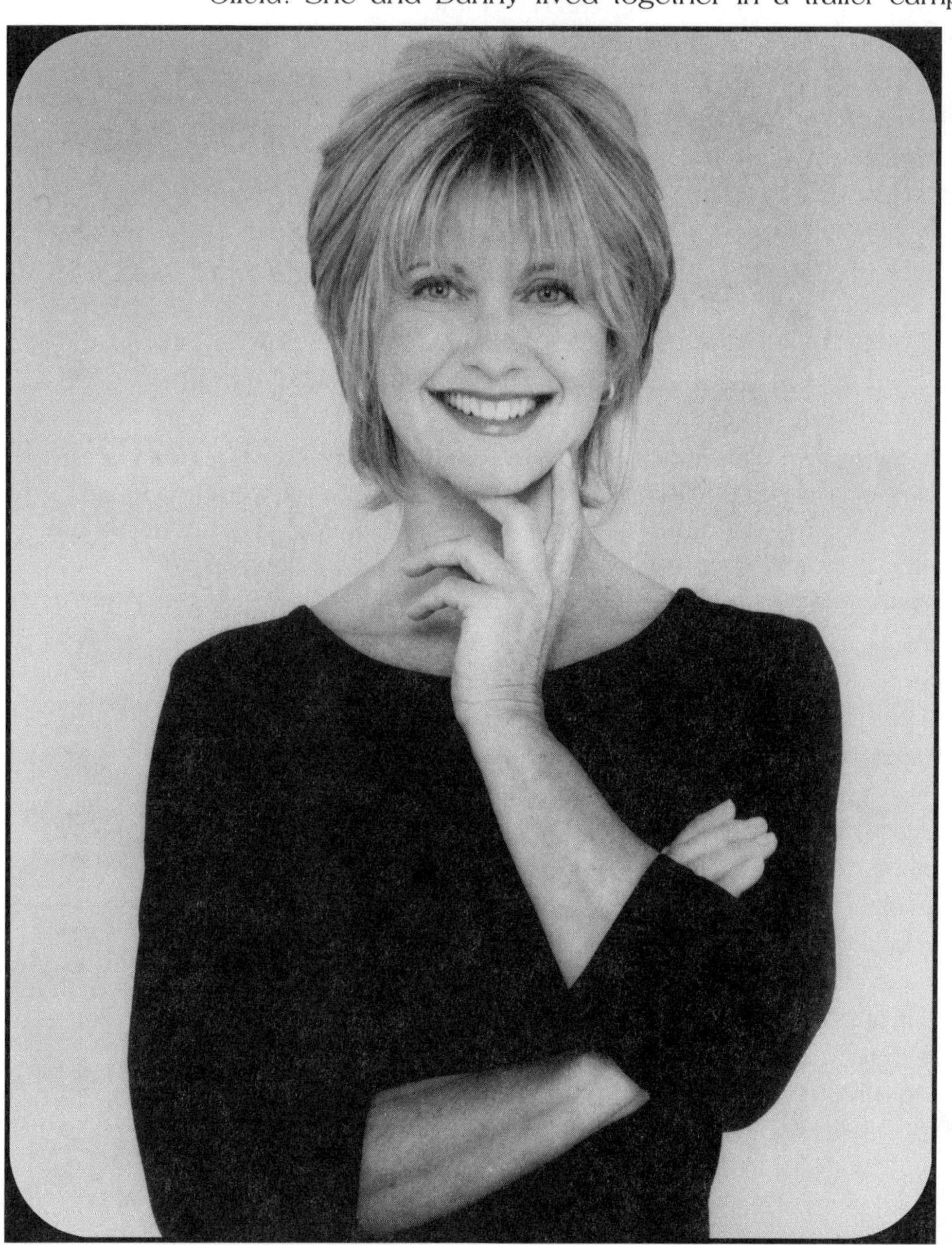

JOHN TRAVOLTA

I LOVE JOHN! Who doesn't? He's an extremely warm and loving friend. I was scheduled to call him after he put his son to sleep at 9:30 in the evening. We talked for over an hour about many interesting topics, both professional and private. While I was listening to John the daddy describe, in his humble and sweet manner, his life with his amazing wife, Kelly, and his beautiful son, Jett, I couldn't help sensing and feeling the magnitude of his success and popularity as John the movie star. It was so palpable that I could hardly sit still. I was very glad I had written out my questions beforehand, because the energy in my office was so great that it was difficult for me to concentrate.

John met Kelly on the set of *The Experts*, a romantic comedy they did together. Says John, "She was married to someone else at the time, and they got divorced about two years later. So by the time she got to me, she was ready to get married for real, you know, not pretend. We got married two different times. First, we got married in Paris at the Ritz Hotel on September 6, 1991. It was unofficial because it was in Paris. When we returned to the United States, we got married again in Daytona on September 13, 1991. So, legally, we were married on the 13th, but spiritually and emotionally, it was September 6th."

I was very interested in John's creative process and what conditions were most conducive to it. "I need everybody to be in a collaborative mode, and I need to be sure that no one will be made to feel wrong or foolish because of ideas they may have. I like it to be fun—literally fun—like, a lot of laughs, because it keeps my spirits up and makes me better in a scene, whether it's dramatic or comedic. It keeps me in neutral, a kind of balanced place from where I can move to either laughter or tears very easily. When you're in neutral, you can most easily go to any gear. And I need to be appropriately worked, not overworked or underworked, just made to put in a decent, respectable day.

"I have to have rehearsals because I believe in them. I think certainty allows a certain kind of creative freedom. If you know the scene backward and forward, you can then throw it away and play with it. But if you don't know it, you spend half your time trying to remember it. I don't like creating by accident. I like kind of knowingly creating. Some wonderful accidents sometimes happen, but they're because you're in a good space to create those accidents, in the right zone. My not liking to 'wing it' could be because of my theater background."

My husband and I had recently seen *Face Off*, and loved the masterful performances of John and Nicolas Cage, and I was very interested to learn how they had prepared for that film. "We rehearsed a lot, we had to, because there was so much that depended on it. Every move that one of us made, the other had to be able to do, too. It had to be seamless. We had to make rehearsals an ethical issue with the studio, because they didn't want us to have any. I said, 'Look, then you shouldn't do this movie, because our performances and the whole outcome of the film is based on Nick and I knowing each other. It would be a joke if we didn't each know exactly what the other is doing and feeling. We've got to decide together what we're going to do here and feel there, what physical things, when we're going to laugh or cry, all that stuff.'"

John is getting ready to do the film adaptation of *A Civil Action*, one of the most gripping and informative nonfiction books I've ever read. It's another fabulous role for John. Coincidentally, I had just heard that Ethan Phillips—the actor who played my husband on "Benson"—has a small part in the film. He is the best joke-teller I know. John won't have to worry about having lots of laughs on that set!

Didi: John, what would Danny Zuko be doing twenty years later?

John: He owns an auto shop that specializes in 1955–57 T-Birds, and on the weekend Sandy and he go out dancing. They have three children.

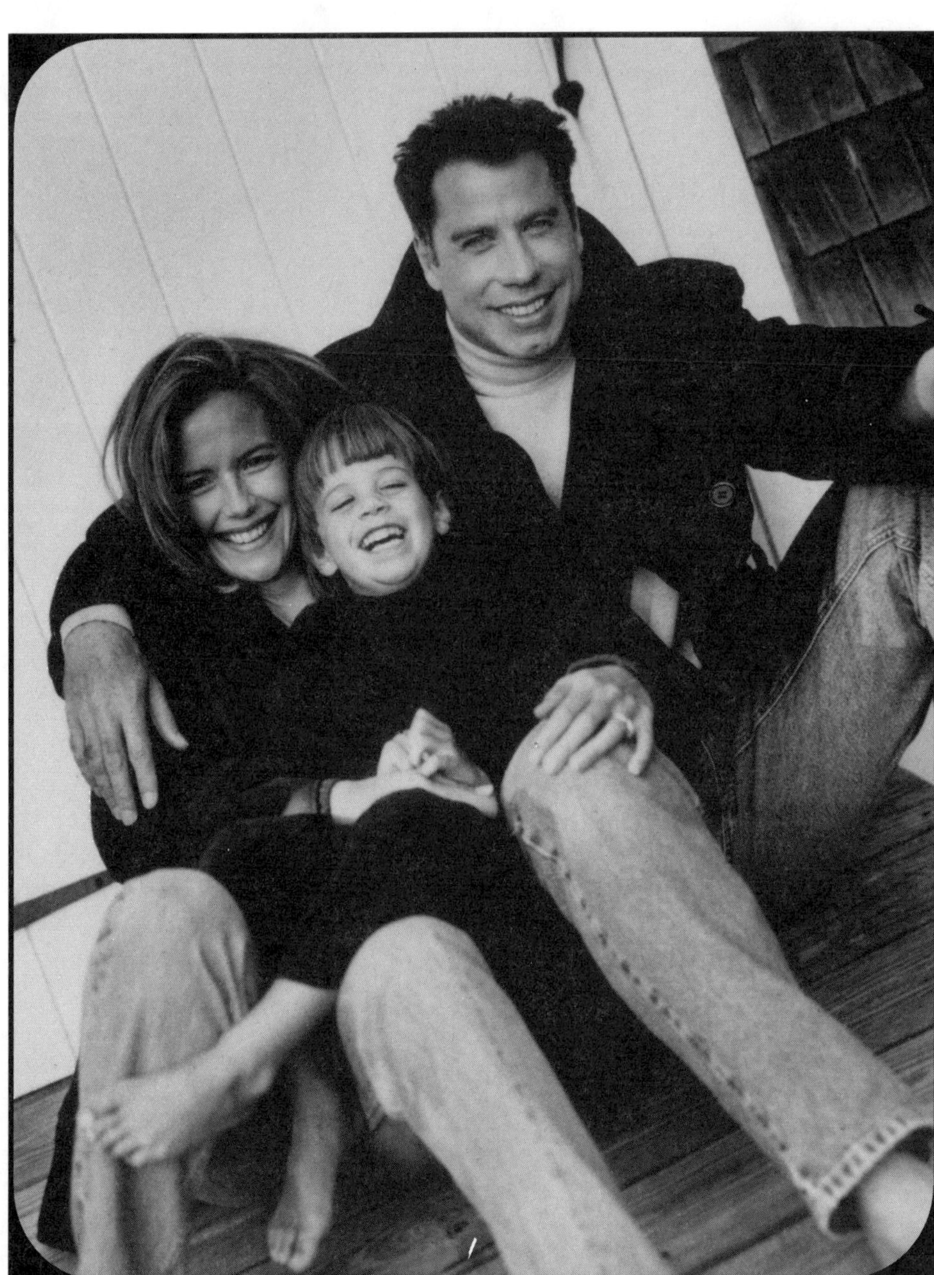

Kelly, Jett, and John.

JEFF CONAWAY

Currently, Jeff is one of the stars of the hit television series "Babylon Five." For the past year he has been commuting between Hollywood and Broadway, where he's been playing Vince Fontaine in a revival of the original stage version of *Grease*.

He told me, "Playing Vince was a very interesting experience. It was like a psychedelic side show—unbelievable. I had to warm up the audience for half an hour before the show began. That was why I took the job. For that half hour Vince Fontaine was it! I was very energetic in the role. I would be off the wall from minute one to minute thirty! The girls went berserk when they saw me. They would be screaming, 'Hey Kenickie!' I would try to stay in the character of Vince, but a couple of times I responded by saying, 'A hickey from Kenickie is like a Hallmark card . . . when you care enough to give the very best!' The place would go insane! I didn't want to do it too much, because the actor playing Kenickie would be up in his dressing room putting on his wig, and he didn't want to hear me on the stage saying his lines! It was a lot of fun. Twenty years ago, when I was starring in *Grease* as Danny Zuko, one night during intermission I turned to my friend Jim Weston and said, joking

Jeff Conaway as Vince Fontaine in the current Broadway production of *Grease.*

around, 'Watch—in twenty years I'm going to be back again playing Vince Fontaine.' Lo and behold, it absolutely happened! And watch, in twenty years I'll be back playing Miss Lynch!"

Jeff is married to a gorgeous woman named Keri.

Didi: What do you think Kenickie would be doing after twenty years?
Jeff: Ah, Kenickie! He became a mechanic, and now he owns a few garages, maybe by now a chain of garages.

Didi: Oh, wow!
Jeff: And he got married to Betty [Rizzo]. And she was definitely the smart one in that marriage! He would have just kept on fixin' and tunin' up cars one at a time and selling them, you know. But it was Betty who figured, Hey, Kenickie, as long as you're going to do this, you should make some money out of it. So she got into the business end, and he just was like a musician—spending all day tinkering with his cars, you know.

Didi: That's beautiful! And do you think he'd have kids?
Jeff: Oh yeah, they'd be screamin' all over the place. There they are kissing, and the kids are always in their face, a constant commotion. Oh, I can just see it! I figure Danny Zuko went to Hollywood and became a movie star. And Betty and Kenickie, I can see them out one night at a drive-in theater, and they're watching one of Danny's films. They're making out in the front seat (as usual—they're always making out!), and they've got six kids howlin' and bawlin' and climbing all over them in their old fixed-up vintage station wagon. And Kenickie opens his eyes for just a second, and he sees that Betty's looking up at the screen, and she's got this, this *look* on her face; and Kenickie says, "Aaaaw, Betty, you *still* got the hots for Zuko!"

STOCKARD CHANNING

Stockard has not stopped working since we filmed *Grease*. She has starred on Broadway numerous times and has won a Tony Award for Best Actress in a Broadway play for *Joe Egg*. Last summer Stockard starred in a Lincoln Center production of *The Little Foxes*, and she was magnificent. She has performed at Lincoln Center numerous times, won a Tony nomination for her riveting and sensitive performance in *Six Degrees of Separation*, and she was also nominated for an Academy Award for her role in the film adaptation. I asked her to tell me about her experience with *Six Degrees*:

"It was great, great . . . fantastic. I mean, it was, like, four years of my life, and I don't know where to begin. I'm so proud of it. But I got to do it, and I got a nomination, which I was very happy about. But with all the publicity and attention I got, people still greet me on the street and say, 'Hi, Rizzo!' I'm still Rizzo after all that!"

Stockard's other film credits include the Paramount film, *The First Wives Club*, *Edie and Pen* for HBO, MGM's *Moll Flanders*, Amblin's *To Wong Foo, Thanks for Everything, Julie Newmar*, *Married to It*, *Meet the Applegates*, *Staying Together*, *Destiny*, *Heartburn*, *The Men's Club*, *The Fortune*, and many more.

Stockard starred in a wonderful film with Harvey Keitel called *Smoke*, which earned her a Golden Globe nomination. The character she played reminded me of Rizzo. "Yes," she said, "I used some of Rizzo in that one. I loved *Smoke*. The character I played could have been Rizzo's aunt.

"I just finished a movie with Paul Newman, called *Magic Hour*. I played his ex-girlfriend and ex-partner, a cop. I walk off into the sunset with him at the end! Unless they changed the ending. He's a divine man in every way, a wonderful guy, gorgeous and so smart. He's great, the best! I'm on my way to do the sequel to a movie called *Unexpected Family*, for which I was nominated for an Emmy. I'm also doing a movie with Laura Dern for Showtime, called *The Baby Dance*, that was written and directed by Jane Anderson."

I asked her the same questions I asked Jeff:

Didi: So what do you think Rizzo would be doing twenty years later?

Stockard: Well, let's see. I always kind of felt like Rydell High was on Long Island, but I assume it must have been in L.A. It was very weird; like I was telling you, sometimes I didn't know how to talk because of all those palm trees around. But twenty years later, I think that Rizzo is definitely living in the Valley. She has a couple of kids, and I think she's probably divorced and, let's see, by now I think she's got her act together, but I think that took her a while.

Didi: Jeff Conaway said an interesting thing about you. He didn't call you Rizzo, he called you Betty, and he talked about how Betty was the sexiest thing and how she really helped Kenickie with his garage.

Stockard: I definitely think that Rizzo and Kenickie got together and that he had a garage. And I think that we must have had a couple of kids, (whispering) but I don't think things worked out very well for them. I think that she finally realized that it was a dysfunctional relationship.

Didi: Conaway told me that Rizzo was the brains behind his business, that it was you that made the garage really work.

Stockard: He's completely in denial. He forgets that I *left* him.

Stockard Channing today (below), in *The Little Foxes* (right), and in *Six Degrees of Separation* (below, right).

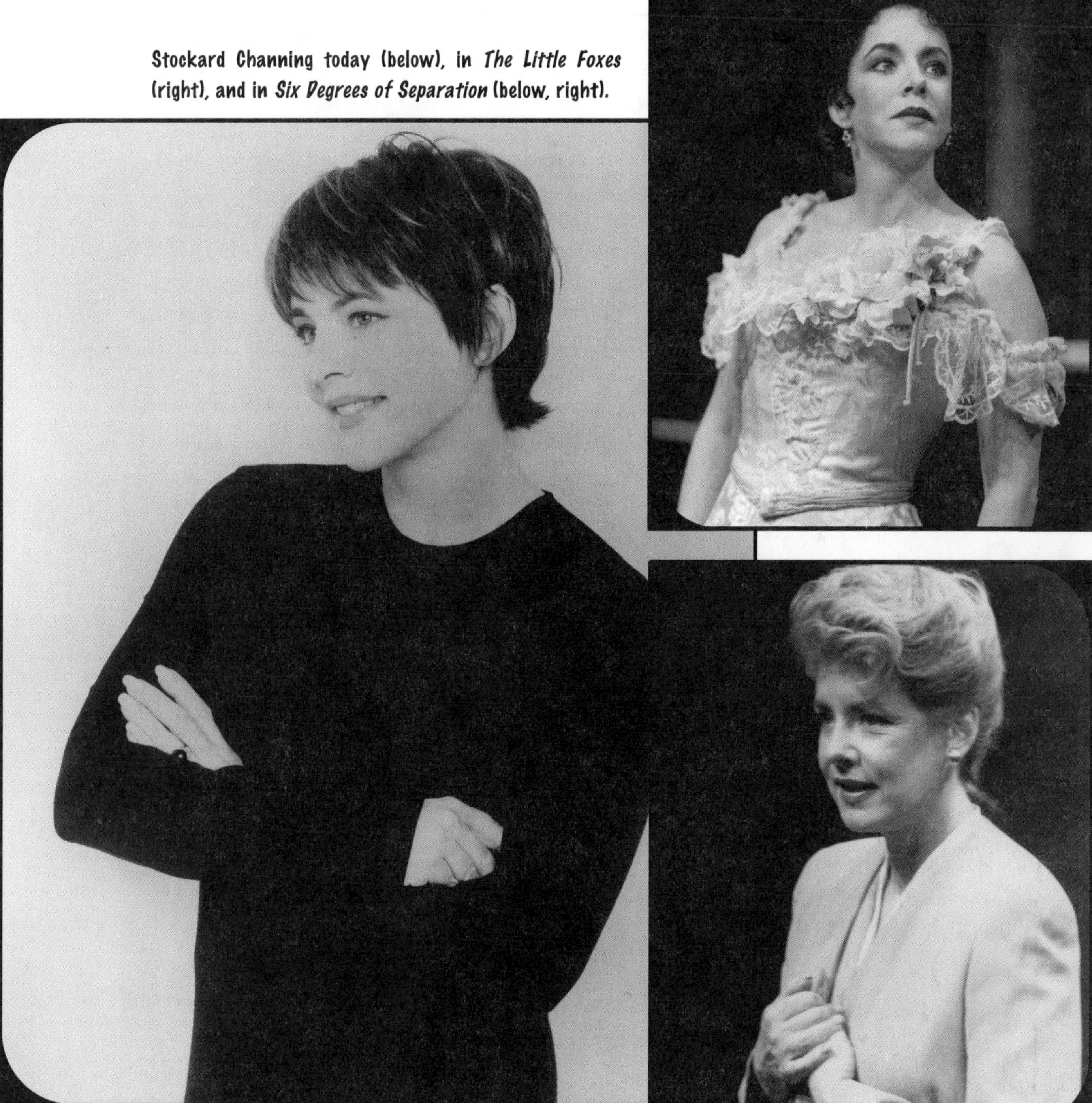

JAMIE DONNELLY

Jamie has been on the road as a personal manager, so it was very hard to reach her. When I finally did, she had a lot to say:

"When I came back to Hollywood in 1996 I was still a writer. I was collaborating with my husband, Stephen Foreman. I came back with two little kids, and I could see the business was in a state of flux. A friend asked me to talk to her daughter about show business and help her with an audition. I helped her a little and she wound up getting the job. Her mother said, 'You know, there are coaches that I'm paying, and everyone pays a fortune to them all the time, and you are better than any of these people.'

"I've always been able to help my friends. Someone would call and say, 'Jamie, I don't know what this director wants from me. Will you read the script and tell me what the hell is going on?' And I would help them. All my life I've understood the perspective of the writer, producer, and actor. I can help these kids. They're so young. They're not embittered, only hopeful and open.

"I really think every actor needs the kind of rehearsal process that you get onstage and never do in film and television. As a coach, I can give them that

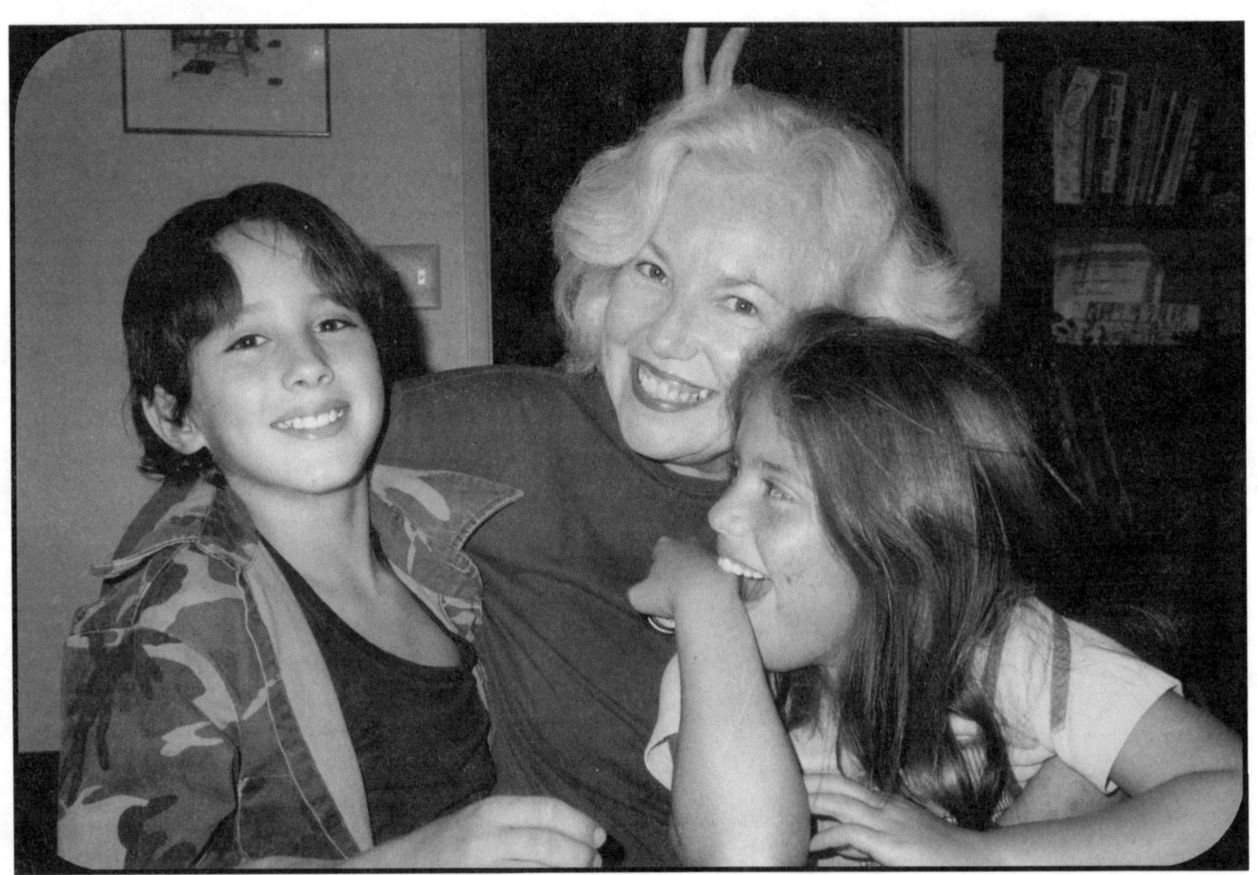

Sevi, Jamie, and Madden Rose.

kind of attention and time, and they are able to do enough work on their part so that by the time they are suddenly in front of the camera they are confident with who they are and who the character is. They feel right, and authentic.

"So that's how I spend my time. I teach young actors and coach them, and I even manage one. Sometimes I'm hired as a coach on a movie if there are a lot of children in the film. I'm managing a very talented young actor named Eric Michael Cole. He's seventeen, from the West, and when he came to L.A., he was living in his car. After he crashed an audition and did very well, an agent called me and asked me to evaluate him. I did, but he needed a lot of care and help, so I had him move in with my family. Within six months he was in *White Squawl*, the Ridley Scott movie. This summer he did *Gia* for HBO and a film for Bob Ackerman in Vancouver in which he plays the bad guy opposite Rob Lowe and Jennifer Grey. So he's real busy, and I'm taking care of him all the time.

"My husband, Stephen, and I have two great kids, Madden Rose, who is eight years old, and Sevi, who is ten. They are from Medellín, Colombia."

Didi: So, Jamie, what would Jan be doing twenty years later?
Jamie: "She'd still be laughing. She had such a great spirit about her, and such a sense of joy and appreciation of other people. She would probably be a great mom, and I think she would always be a happy and satisfied person. I never saw Jan as an intellectual or a person with any particularly unique gifts. I always hoped that girls in the audience would be able to look at her and say, "'That's kind of what *I'm* like." Over the years I've had a lot of people say to me, "I really identified with your character; I always felt like her." I think all the Pink Ladies had that—we all sort of play different parts of what makes up a young woman. Different people might relate more to one or another of us, but I think that Jan is like so many of us and like so many girls of any time or any age who just have a time in their lives where being part of the gang is more important than anything else in the world to them.

Didi: And later on in life?
Jamie: I think she would have focused all that "belonging" energy on her family—because, for Jan, it was always much more about love than about style.

Didi: So, she'd be a mom.
Jamie: Yeah, I think she would. And I think she might have gotten married to Putzie.

KELLY WARD

"I segued into being a writer, and it has opened lots of doors to directing and producing, predominately in the area of animated entertainment. The first feature I wrote was called *Once Upon A Forest*. I made it with animator/producer Charles Grosvenor and writer Mark Young. We made it for Hanna Barbera, but it was released by Twentieth Century Fox. It went from being a six-hundred-thousand-dollar television movie to a sixteen-million-dollar feature film!

"Mark and I coproduced a number of different projects on a number of different levels. We coproduced an entire canon of Pink Panther cartoons and a feature short with the Pink Panther. Also, we coproduced a sequel to the movie *All Dogs Go to Heaven* entitled *All Dogs Go to Heaven 2*. It was fun. It took us to exotic places all over the world. I directed all the actors and produced the song vocals with songwriters Barry Mann and Cynthia Weil. That was wonderful. Most recently, I'm working at Disney Studios voice-directing a syndicated series based on *101 Dalmatians*. I have been working on *Casper*, an animated series for Universal, as well. So I have a lot of contact and interaction with actors, which has always been my favorite thing to do, both as an actor and a director.

"I met my beautiful wife Annette in 1974 doing a production of *Fiddler on the Roof*. We have three amazing boys. Garrett is nine, Matt is fourteen, and Nik is seventeen. They're

Kelly and Annette.

NO PARKING
AT ANY TIME
Barry Pearl
Michael Tucci
Kelly Ward

PANAVISION

RYDELL

STOP

musicians, athletes, and artists—great kids, stimulating and intelligent, and they're not in trouble! We have been very lucky, and hopefully we've done something right. They're good boys and all enjoy a certain celebrity amongst their friends because of my participation in *Grease*. Their dad is Putzie! What cracks me up is, I'll be driving along the road and I'll see a car come alongside, and when we stop for a light, the kids in the car next to me will say, 'Fifteen minutes!' I think, what are they talking about? And then I realize they're saying one of Putzie's funny lines from *Grease*!"

Didi: So, Kelly, what do you think ol' Putzie would be doing twenty years later?
Kelly: Well, I know one thing for sure.

Didi: *What's that?*
Kelly: My own kids have turned out to be *much* cooler than Putzie ever was!

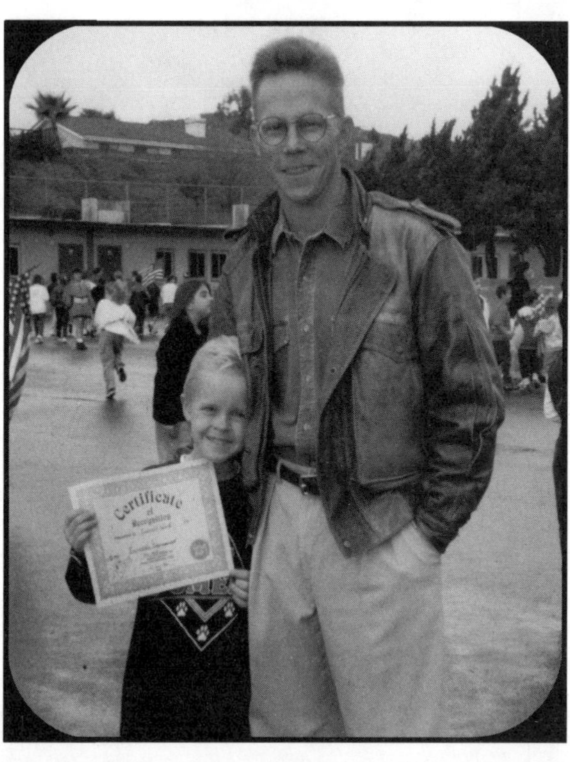

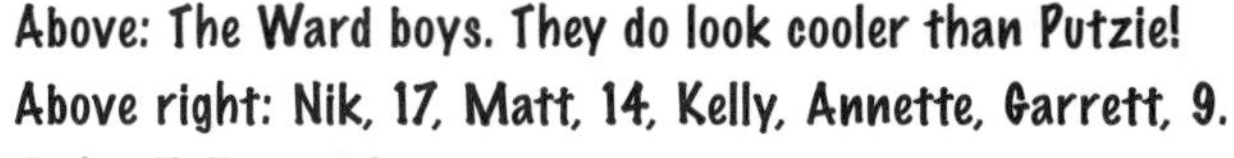

Above: The Ward boys. They do look cooler than Putzie!
Above right: Nik, 17, Matt, 14, Kelly, Annette, Garrett, 9.
Right: Kelly and Garrett.

DINAH MANOFF

Dinah has two new men in her life. The handsome big guy is Arthur Mortell and the delicious little guy is their five-month-old baby boy, Dashiel Manoff Mortell.

Dinah told me her pregnancy was pretty great, except for the last month, which they don't tell you about in the books. "I thought it was probably the most horrific month in my life! They always say you are pregnant for nine months. You're not. You are pregnant for ten! The tenth month is hell!! You hate everybody, and you think the baby will never come. You don't know why you ever did this in the first place. And then it's over and it's fabulous—you got your prize. I am so in love with this little boy!"

Dinah also told me about an exciting new direction that her career has been taking. "I started directing when I was on the sitcom 'Empty Nest.' I directed a bunch of our shows, and then last year I directed some other four-camera shows. I love directing four-camera; I think it's such a hoot. But my favorite thing is to direct live theater. That's the best—there's nothing more fun than that. Directing four cameras is like directing theater with testosterone—you know what I mean? It's a very powerful job and a lot of fun. I also directed a show for UPN called 'Minor Adjustments,' and I directed an episode of 'Sister, Sister.'"

Now Dinah is mostly writing because she is at home with her baby boy. Just this last year she wrote two screenplays.

Didi: Dinah, what do you think Marty would be doing twenty years later?
Dinah: Oh God! What a good question! (laughter) I think I've got it—I think she would be married to Sonny. And I think she would gain fifty pounds, which would make her much more voluptuous. She would be an impeccable dresser with a real sense of style, and lots of jewelry. And I think that she would have, oh, three kids, and be a real kind of PTA mom who eats a lot of chocolate! (more laughter) And she would be very loyal to Sonny. I wonder what Sonny would be doing; I can't wait to hear what (Michael) Tucci has to say about him. That's so funny!

Didi: Any other thoughts?
Dinah: I really just see her married to Sonny, I really do.

Didi: So did Tucci . . .
Dinah: "He did, too?"

Didi: Oh, yes. Married to Marty!
Dinah: Marty and Sonny—they just kind of belonged together.

Didi: And what about Vince Fontaine? Did he ever come around again?
(Dinah only giggled!)

Dinah Manoff (right), and with son, Dashiel, and Arthur Mortell (below).

MICHAEL TUCCI

Michael Tucci told me he is married to a "spectacular" woman named Kathleen Sawyer. They have two wonderful kids, Kelly, two and a half, and Kate, eight. He is currently one of the stars of the television series "Diagnosis Murder." I asked him about the jobs he's enjoyed doing the most these last twenty years.

"Well, right after *Grease*, I signed with CBS and I did three pilots for them. Then we did 'Paper Chase,' and I played Gerald Golden, president of the Harvard Law Issue. 'Paper Chase' became a very underground kind of cult series. Then I did 'It's Garry Shandling's Show,' and I played Pete Schumacher, Gary's best friend, and we did that show for five years. It was the first series on Showtime to win the Best Series Award and the Pace Award. Then the show was moved to Fox and ran five more years. Then I did two seasons of 'Flying Blind,' with Tea Leoni playing my son's girlfriend. And now there is 'Diagnosis Murder.' I play Norman Briggs, the administrator of the hospital. We're going into our sixth year. So basically, it's been seventeen years of television."

Didi: What do you think Sonny would be doing twenty years later?
Michael: He'd own a pizzeria and be a millionaire.

Didi: Do you have a name for his pizzeria?
Michael: Well, what would Sonny and Marty call it? Oh, S & M, Sonny and Marty, S & M Pizza! That's it; that would be just like them—a little bit off-color, just their sense of humor. And it would be a beautiful, classy place, full of character, like a place I know in Boston that makes the best pizza in the world. Lots of character and everything high quality and really tasty. You know, the old coal stoves, the beautiful crusts, the special sauce from the recipe passed down from Marty's grandparents—just the best, breathtaking, beautiful pizza.

Didi: And would you have franchises, do you think, or just the one place in Brooklyn?
Michael: No, I'd think there would be a couple of S & Ms—not a million, maybe just two or three. But really classy—people coming from all over the world just to have a taste of Sonny's pizza. Yeah, Sonny would really like that. So he would own a pizzeria. He'd drive a Cadillac. His kids would go to Catholic school. And Marty—she would always be in style. Marty would be like the Imelda Marcos of wherever they live—her neighborhood is like her own little empire, and she's got a zillion pairs of shoes and a classy wardrobe. And they *never* cheat on each other. Never!

Didi: Are you sure about that?
Michael: I'm sure. Marty kinda sowed all her wild oats before she got married, and now she's really happy to be settled down. And Sonny? He's a real straight-ahead guy.

Didi: Doesn't Vince Fontaine come around looking for Marty every once in a while?
Michael: Well, maybe. But that's just titillation.

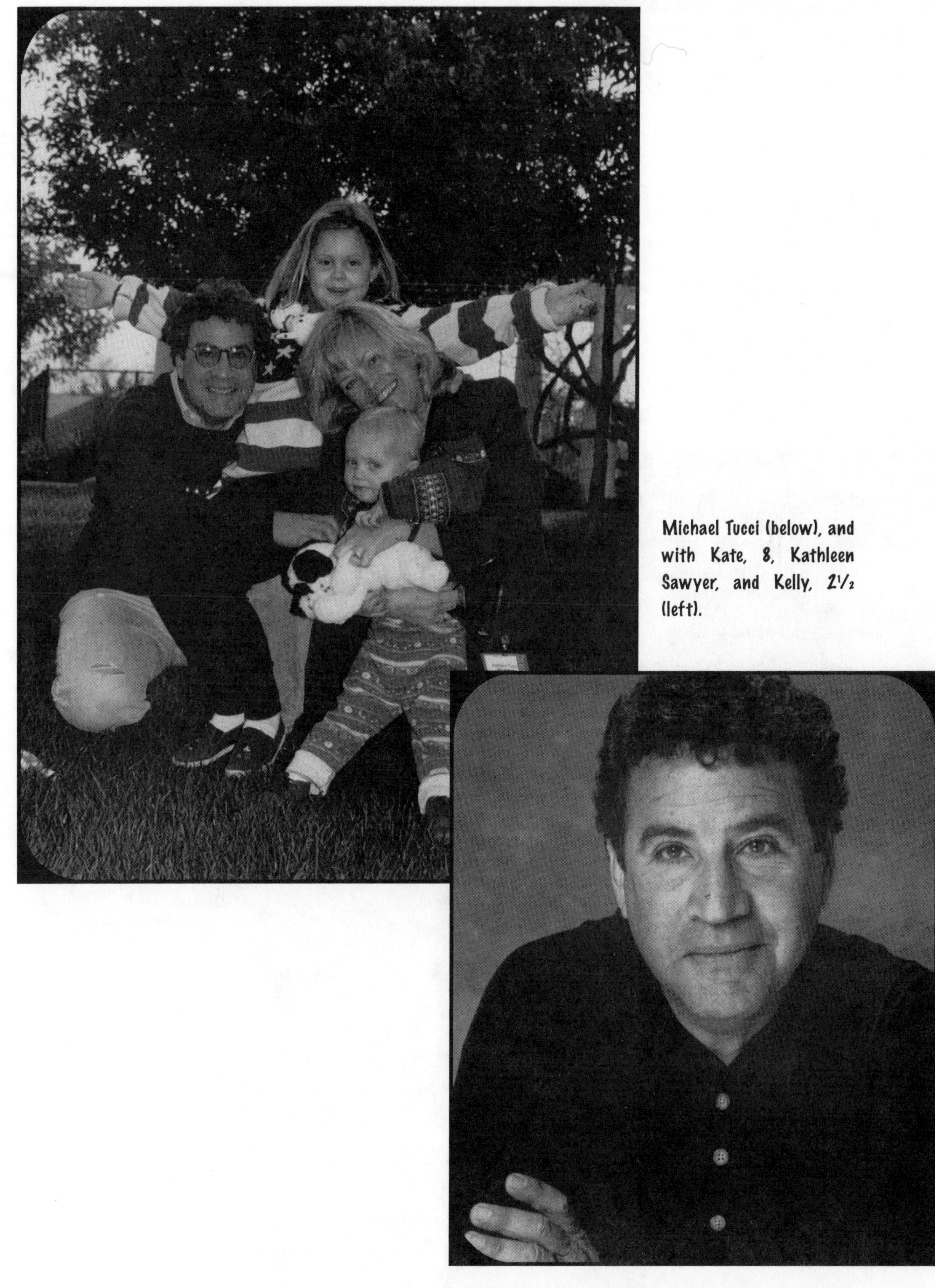

Michael Tucci (below), and with Kate, 8, Kathleen Sawyer, and Kelly, 2½ (left).

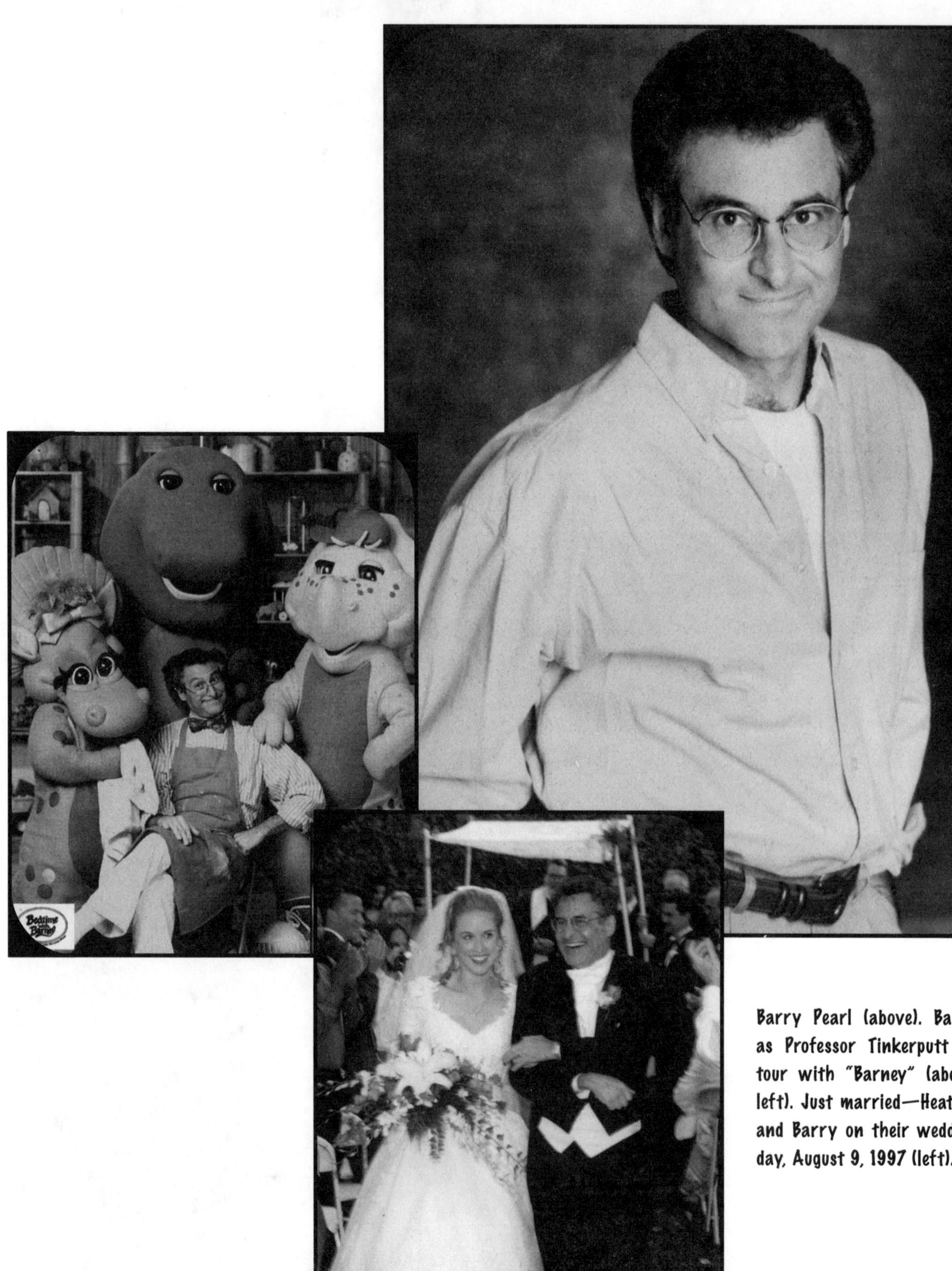

Barry Pearl (above). Barry as Professor Tinkerputt on tour with "Barney" (above, left). Just married—Heather and Barry on their wedding day, August 9, 1997 (left).

BARRY PEARL

"*Grease* will always be one of the highlights of my career. It was such a labor of love. The next role that was as much fun to do in front of a camera was the part of Professor Erasmus Q. Tinkerputt in a 'Barney' prime-time special. Now we're doing a live stage show, *Barney's Big Surprise*. Professor Tinkerputt uses his imagination to invent all kinds of exciting toys in his toy factory. It is extremely gratifying work. We work in theaters that seat six thousand children. When Barney comes out on the stage, these kids raise the roof!

"I met my beautiful wife, Heather, last summer during a production of *Guys and Dolls*. I was playing Nathan Detroit, and she was one of the Hot Box Girls. July fourth of 1996, I asked her out and we dated casually, and by the time I left to do the Barney show, she took me to the airport, and I said I'll send you a postcard. I get out on tour and I miss her and she starts missing me, and over the phone we decide we can't live without each other. I'm sure I was one of Sprint's biggest customers last year. On Christmas Eve, in front of all the family, I asked her to marry me. I went and bought a diamond on West Forty-Seventh Street in New York. We got married on August 9, 1997. Now she's in the Barney show, too!"

Didi: So what do you think old Doody would be doing twenty years later?
Barry: I've been thinking about that. First, I think Doody wanted to be a stand-up comic. And he went around to the local saloons, and he studied and he practiced, and he tried, and he failed at it. He wasn't real good, so he wound up becoming a used car salesman. It was either that or selling shoes, because his father was a shoe salesman. And he had this dumb joke he'd always tell about how he almost went into the *shoe* business because it was close to *show* business. So he worked with his dad for a while, but shoes just weren't his thing. He was really itching to get out there and schmooze people. So he wound up becoming a used car salesman.

Didi: I can see the sign in front of the dealership: Doody Del Fuego Motors. And did he get married?
Barry: Yes, he got married and had a lot of kids. A lot of kids! Hey, you know, he's Italian, and he wound up marrying an Italian girl. And he's into it at first, but after a while, it kind of overwhelms him. It almost breaks him—because he has this bunch of kids, seven kids, oh, my God! All these little Doodys running around! And he was a real anal-retentive type, like I am, totally anal-compulsive, so he always wanted to have everything orderly and in control. But by the time he had these seven children, he completely gave up his obsession with neatness. Because he just couldn't keep things in order with that many kids. But at Del Fuego Motors, he's still a real operator, a real character. Maybe he'll even try stand-up again!

FRANKIE AVALON

I reached Frankie at his home in California, and it was great to hear that wonderful voice again:

"I do a lot of traveling all over the world, and you just can't believe the impact of *Grease*! I'm from the fifties generation, right? That's when it started, forty years ago, believe it or not! But because of that picture and that song and our scene, I am now known by seven-, eight-, and nine-year-olds, and another generation that's twenty, twenty-two, and still another that's now forty. And then there are the people who grew up with me, and on and on and on! When I was on the set rehearsing for those six days, I could just feel it. It reminded me very much of the same kind of a feeling we had when we did our successful group of pictures, the 'Beach Party' films. It was the same kind of feeling. We all had a great time, like we did on *Grease*.

My teen angel also told me about a new cookbook of his that's just come out. Here's one of his special angel-hair recipes:

Remember when, as Frenchy, I was so confused and wished I had a guardian angel to tell me what to do? And then, Frankie appears and gives me some unexpected advice. Now, twenty years later, I asked Frankie to give today's teenagers some heavenly tips:

Frankie Avalon on body piercing:
"I don't think anyone should fool around or puncture their body. You know, I don't think that that's the thing to do. To me, it's a fad, and hopefully it will be gone very soon. I don't advise it for anybody."

Frankie Avalon on torn clothing:
"You know, my mother always said to me, 'Be neat and clean, and make sure your shoes are polished and your teeth are clean, and then you can go anywhere.' Oh, yeah, and clean underwear!"

Frankie Avalon's heavenly prediction for the future of today's teenagers:
"I predict that kids will become closer to their families. I think kids will want to spend more time with their parents. There was one generation there that just wanted to get away from them, as far away as they could. I think kids now will want to stay close to their moms and dads."

Frankie's Fresh "Teen Angel"-Hair Tomato Sauce

3–4	Cloves of garlic, diced or sliced
1	Small onion, chopped
4–5	Italian tomatoes, cut up
5–6	Fresh basil leaves
2	Tablespoons of olive oil or cooking spray

In a skillet with olive oil or cooking spray, add onions and garlic and sauté appoximately five minutes. Add tomatoes and basil. Place lid on skillet halfway and simmer over low heat for fifteen minutes. Cowabunga!!

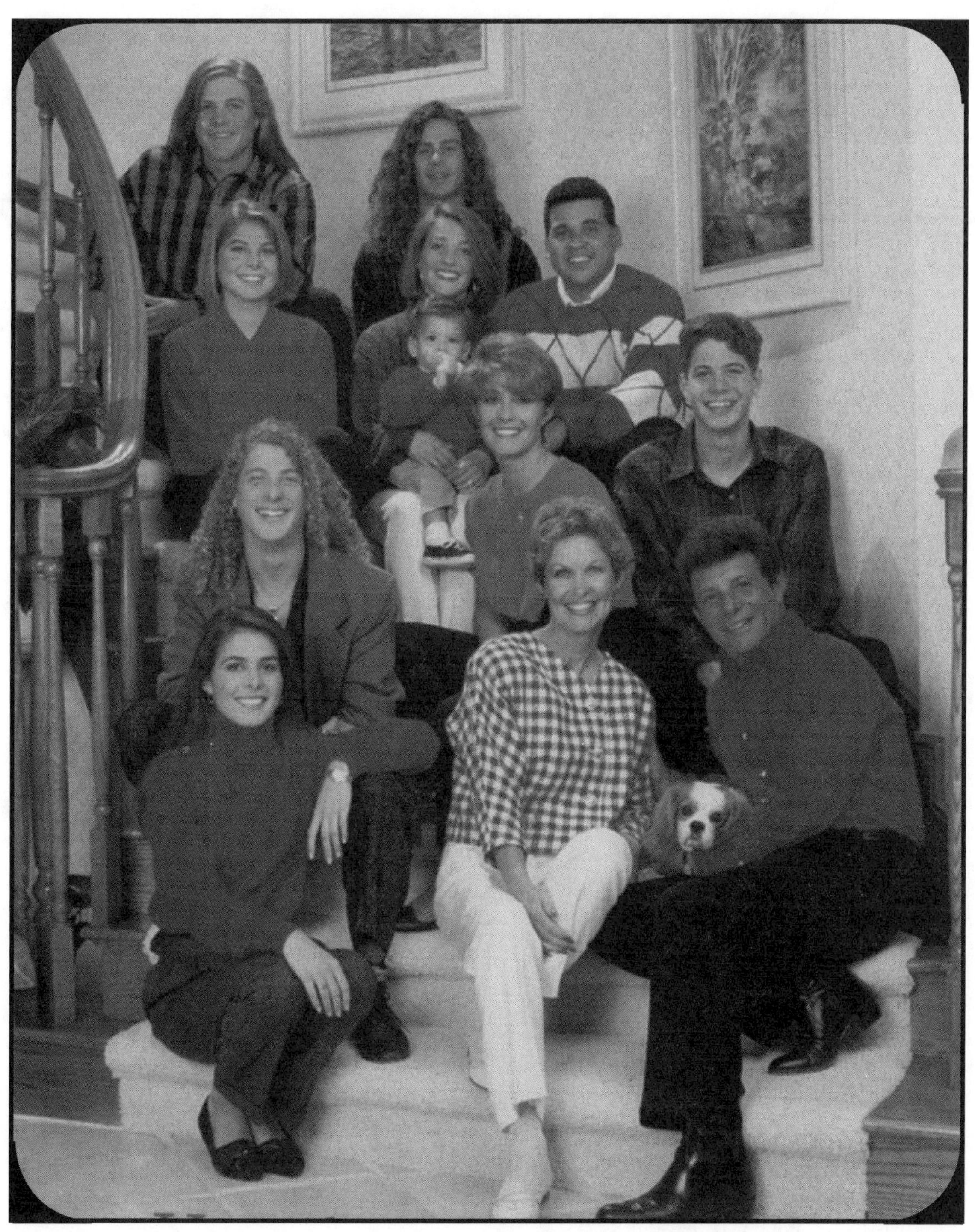

Frankie and Kay Avalon & family.

ANNETTE CARDONA

I met Annette a few years ago at a dry cleaner's on Ventura Boulevard in Sherman Oaks, California. She told me about a dance class she was teaching two nights a week just a few blocks away. I took the class and it was fantastic. It was sexy, fiery, passionate modern jazz and flamenco all rolled together. Annette is an amazing teacher. One night I arrived early, and I opened the classroom door to see three middle-aged women in leotards having a private class with Annette. I excused myself for intruding and waited outside. Around ten minutes later, the door to the studio opened, and three middle-aged *men* in suits came out. Needless to say, I was a bit confused.

Then Annette explained that one year before men who want to become women have their surgery, they have to prepare by spending a certain amount of time dressing and acting like women. Movement is a very significant part of the preparation for people who are making this transition.

Annette told me more:

"I also did a PBS special on movement and transsexuals. It's called *Gabby*, and it follows the life of one of the transsexuals. Gabby talks about how she came to my movement class, and she's very funny. She talks about the day when I told her, 'TUCK IT IN! TUCK IT IN! COME ON, GABBY, TUCK IT IN!' She thought I meant she should tuck in her penis, when, of course, I meant her belly! What a miscommunication! Since then I published an article in a scientific medical journal about my work and the men going through this incredible transition.

"I have been a college professor for the last four years, teaching performing arts, and currently I'm on the faculty of Santa Monica College. When I walk into a classroom, the students still recognize me to this day. I talk about *Grease* with them, how we made the movie, how we did it, how we worked as actors. I use my experience playing Cha Cha as a vehicle to teach them about commitment and passion. There are so many examples from *Grease* that I can utilize without just glorifying my own part in it.

"Wherever I go, people recognize me. Kids who were not even born when we shot the movie have grown up on the *Grease* videotape, and their children watch it every day. They just can't believe I'm the same person. They tell me how much they liked the part and how they memorized it. They recreate my hairdo and costumes at home, just for fun. They can't get over how well I've stayed in shape and how I'm really much nicer in person than Cha Cha, even though they love her feistiness.

"I was just recently in Englewood, New Jersey, and I was walking down a street with a friend when this man came running out of a building screaming at me. It turned out he was a hairdresser doing some lady's hair, and he saw me through the window, left his client in the chair, ran out into the street and said, 'It can't be, it just can't be!' Cha Cha was his favorite character, and he loved my hairdos in the film. He was just so happy to meet me! *Grease* makes people happy, and it seems that the intensity of that happiness doesn't end."

Didi: What do you think Cha Cha would be doing twenty years later?
Annette: Oh! Probably running a dance studio, bossing everybody around. And being *very* passionate.

Didi: Do you think she's married?
Annette: Many times over, I'd say!

Didi: And children?
Annette: Oh, yeah, probably a couple of little Cha Chas—Chachitas! They'd kind of have to dress just like their mom—kind of fiery. And they like to hang out at the dance studio and act bossy like their mom. They turn on the tape deck and start the warm-ups when Cha Cha's late starting class. Maybe they're even twins.

Didi: You know, Annette, I could almost see Cha Cha doing some of the same amazing dance therapy work that you've been doing in your own career.
Annette: With her passion, and her unconventional and very worldly ways of thinking, I could really see Cha Cha doing work like that.

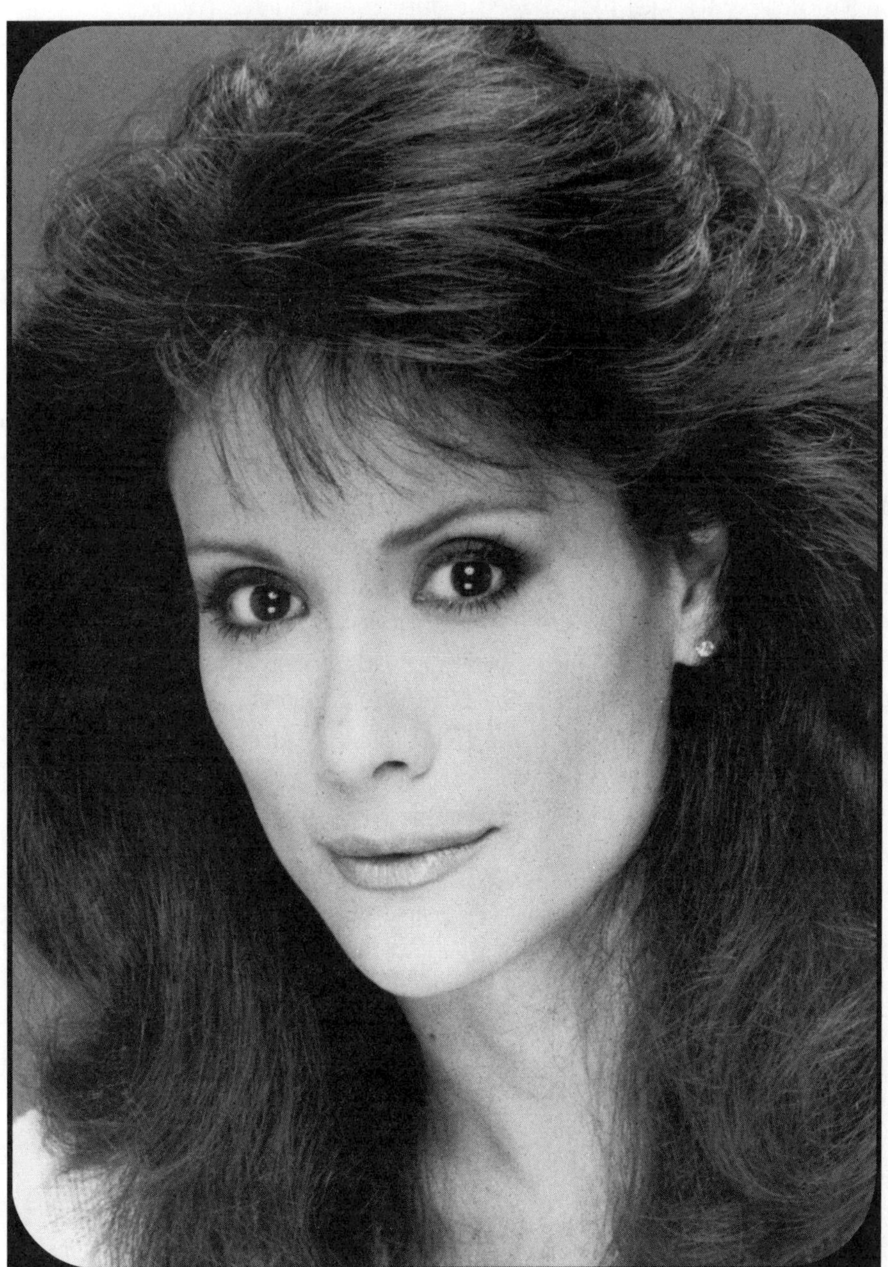

Annette Cardona.

SUSAN BUCKNER

I was so happy to finally reach Susan because I had been calling the wrong number for a month! I just had to try information one more time, and at last I found her. I also spoke to her daughter, Samantha, who sounded so confident and self-assured. Susan and her family live in Miami, where she is starting a new life. Here's what she told me:

"It's exciting. I am doing a lot of new things. I still love to dance and I love music, so I am currently teaching an aerobics dance class. It's all choreographed to funky rock music and a lot of fun. I got involved with a concert dance company called the Miami Movement Dance Company. The choreographer is a creative genius. I promoted and managed them before the choreographer left the company and moved to New York.

"I am recognized all the time by kids. I definitely win their vote when they discover I was Patty Simcox. At Halloween, some of them would rather have autographs and pictures than candy. Some people I meet on the street just start reciting my lines for me. They really get into it, and they're good, too! Everybody wants to know what John Travolta was like.

"I am now a single mother of two great kids. Adam is sixteen and driving. Samantha is thirteen and wants to be an actress. I don't get a chance to volunteer for anything because my kids always volunteer for me first. When Adam was ten, he pulled me into his drama club at elementary school. They were doing a full production of *Grease*. I was just going to help with a couple of scenes, but I ended up directing and choreographing the whole thing. I've been doing a show for the drama club every year since, even though my kids have moved on. I'm very proud of the finished products. They look more like high school productions than elementary school. I'm crazy for special effects. We've put on *The Wizard of Oz, Bye Bye Birdie, The Secret Garden, The Little Mermaid*, and *Beauty and the Beast*. Adam had lead roles in two shows, and Samantha got to star in two of them as well."

Didi: Susan, what do you think Patty Simcox would be doing twenty years later?
Susan: Patty would definitely be a Mary Kay salesperson with the pink Cadillac for high sales. She does everything perfectly. She is the PTA president, and her kids are involved in every activity their school has to offer. She dresses perfectly conservative. I think, though, that she's a closet drinker. Maybe she paid a little visit to Betty Ford's and got thrown out for trying to sell the other ladies cosmetics!

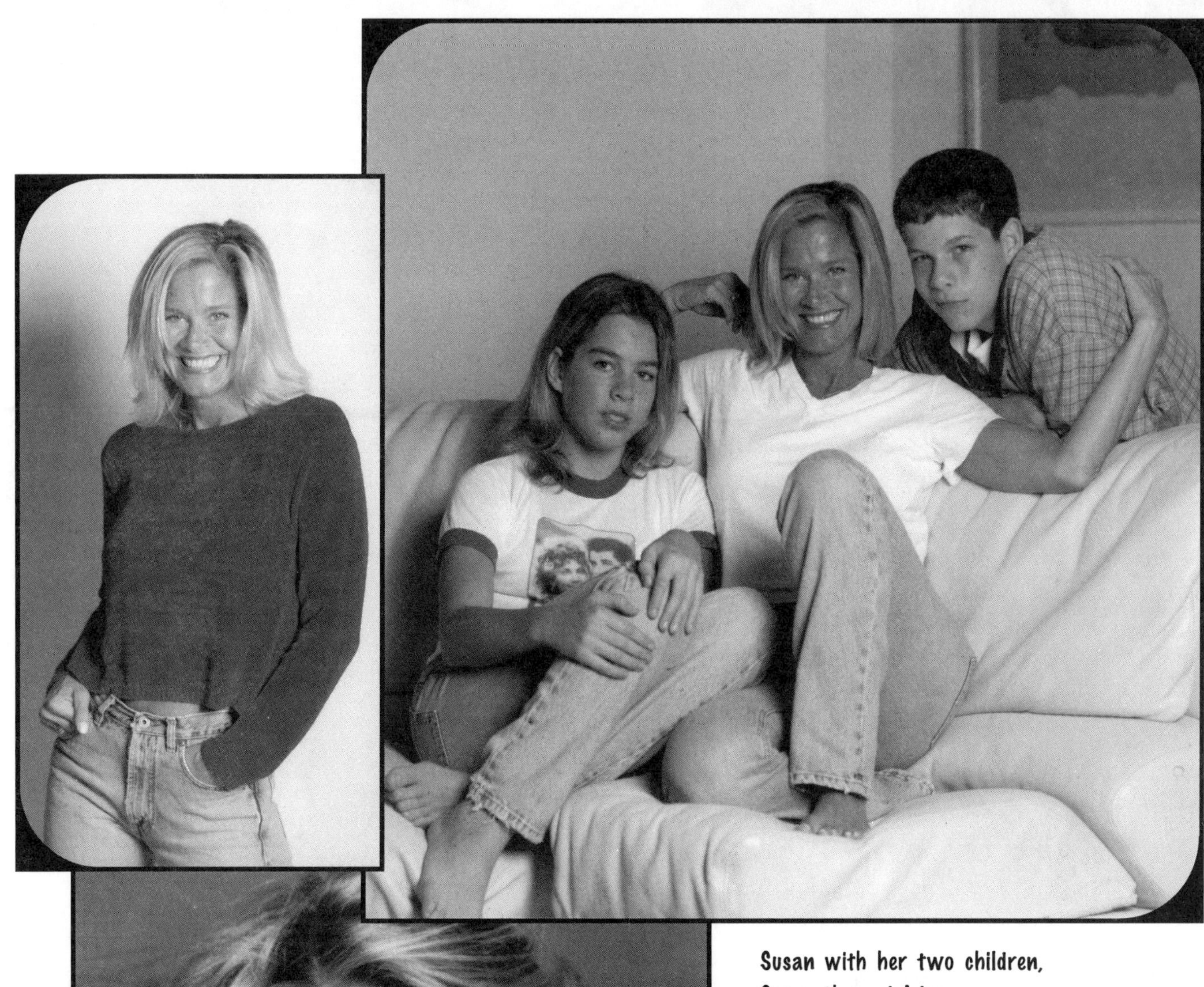

Susan with her two children, Samantha and Adam.

LORENZO LAMAS

Lorenzo met his stunning wife, Shauna, on the set of *Renegade*, a show he was doing in San Diego.

"She was working on the set one day," he told me, "and we started talking and *boom*! I had been divorced for a year and a half and I didn't think I was ever going to remarry. I had come to the conclusion that maybe I was not cut out for marriage because I had such terrible luck. I was just going to concentrate on raising my three kids, a thirteen-year-old boy named A.J., an eleven-year-old daughter, Shayne, and an eight-year-old daughter, Paton. But everything comes into focus when you meet the one who really came from the same planet as you. I thank God I met Shauna when I was still young enough to be able to spend most of my life with her. We are expecting our first baby in December, and we've already named her Alexandra Lyn. I am very excited!"

Didi: So what do you think old Tommy would be doing twenty years later?
Lorenzo: He'd have taken over for Coach Calhoun; he'd be coaching football at Rydell High.

Didi: Of course he would! And do you think he'd have gotten married?
Lorenzo: Oh, sure. He's probably got five kids. Tom was a sweet, kind of slightly stupid, innocent young kid. So I think probably he would end up marrying the homecoming queen, living a very normal life—Mr. Happily Ever After.

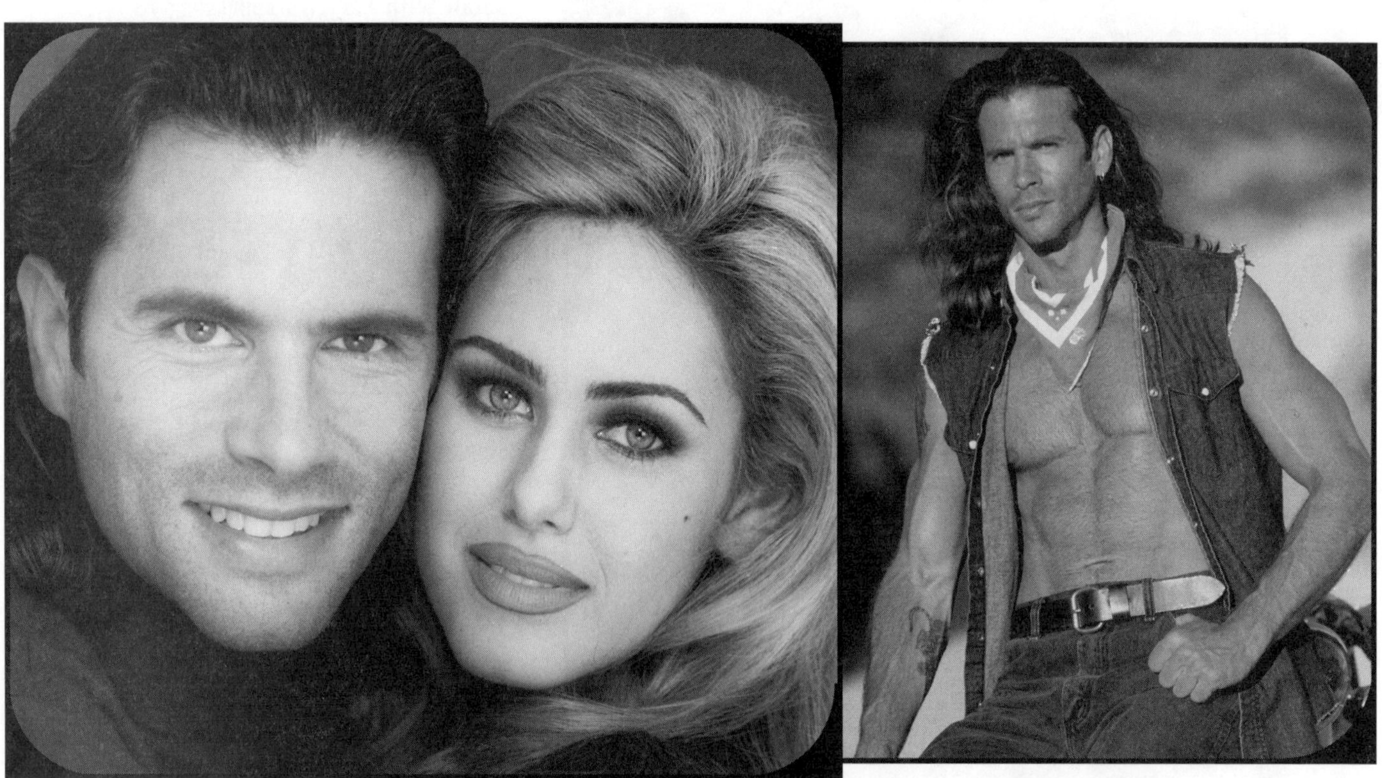

Lorenzo and Shauna Sand, his gorgeous wife (left), and on the set of *Renegade* (right).

DODY GOODMAN

When I reached Dody, she was getting ready to go off to Spain to do a recycling commercial for Pepsi-Cola. Dody was on Broadway last year playing Miss Lynch in *Grease*. She played Miss Lynch in the road company of *Grease* as well. Last summer, Dody starred in *Social Security* in summer stock. Also, Dody starred in *Nunsense*, as Sister Mary Amnesia, in the national tour. She is currently playing the Reverend Mother in *Nunsense* at the Helen Hayes Performing Arts Center in Nyack, New York.

Didi: I'm glad to know what Dody Goodman is doing twenty years later. But now, tell me, what would Blanche be doing?

Dody: I guess she'd probably be retired from her job by now. She wasn't a teacher; she was a worker for Eve Arden at Rydell High. She was a clever woman, a schemer, always fixing things, working things out behind the scenes. So once she retired, I'm sure she'd be looking for something creative to devote her full energy to. Community theater! That's it! She just got finished playing Yenta in *Fiddler on the Roof* at the Jewish Community Center. She got a good write-up in the neighborhood block association's monthly newsletter, and now she's got the bug. She'll *never* quit!

Dody as Sister Mary Amnesia in *Nunsense* (right). "Blanche" as Yenta in *Fiddler on the Roof* (left).

ALICE GHOSTLEY

Alice and her lovely husband, Felice Orlandi, have lived in Studio City, California, since 1969. In the early 1980s, she starred on Broadway in *Annie* as Miss Hannigan. Alice has guest-starred on hundreds of television shows. She starred in the hit series *Designing Women* for seven years.

Didi: Now that it is twenty years later, do you think Miss Murdock has retired?
Alice: Oh, no! She taught auto mechanics for another ten years at Rydell. Then she decided she wanted to make more money, so she moved to Detroit and got a job at Ford Motors, working on the ground level explaining to visiting tourists how a car is built. But here's a little secret: with all her love for cars, Miss Murdoch doesn't know how to drive! She took fifty-five driving lessons—finally got her license, and on her first outing ran into a tree, took off the side of her car, and said, "That's it! This is not for me." She has several citations from the Department of Motor Vehicles for her excellent driving record, but that's because she has never driven a car since!

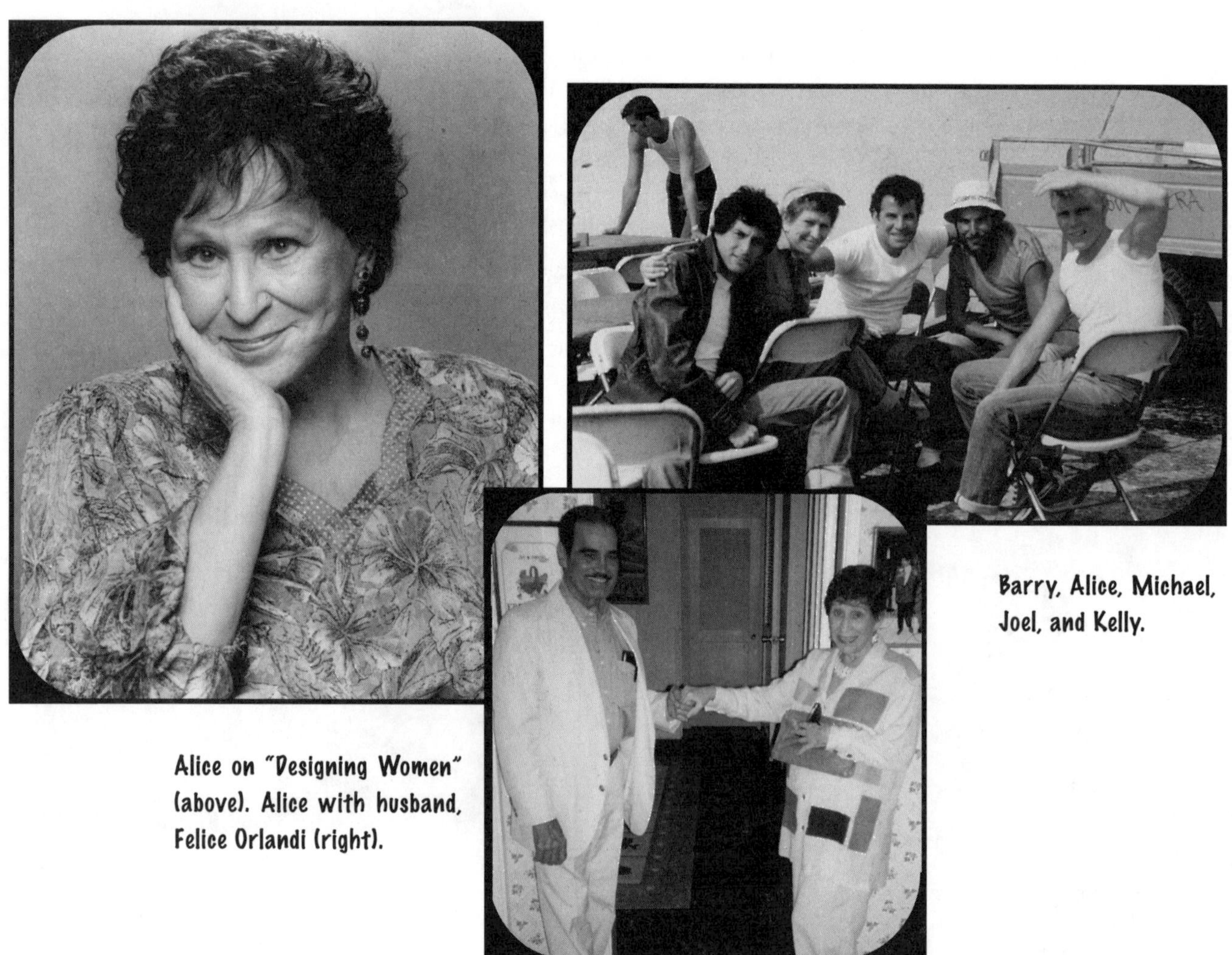

Barry, Alice, Michael, Joel, and Kelly.

Alice on "Designing Women" (above). Alice with husband, Felice Orlandi (right).

DICK PATTERSON

It took me a while to find Dick because he and his wife, Pat Lynn, were on the road. Here is an excerpt from a letter Dick wrote to me:

"Here we are in our new motor home. I'm retired from show biz. I had to leave because of illness and fatigue—yeah!—they got sick and tired of me! Ho, ho, ho! Pat and I are enjoying our traveling life—seeing the great U.S.A., Las Vegas, the Great Salt Lake, Glacier National Park, (the site of) Custer's Last Stand, Mount Rushmore, Devil's Tower, etc., etc. What a beautiful country this is! I'm back in my old hometown, Clear Lake, Iowa, for my *fiftieth* high school reunion. The class of 1947! Wow! We had forty-six out of fifty-one classmates attend—not bad, huh? In appreciation of all my hard work in organizing the reunion, they gave me my own letterman's jacket. Coach Calhoun would be proud!"

Didi: What do you think Mr. Rudie would be doing twenty years later?

Dick: Mr. Rudie is living in Clear Lake, Iowa, working at the famous Surf Ballroom teaching the "hand jive."

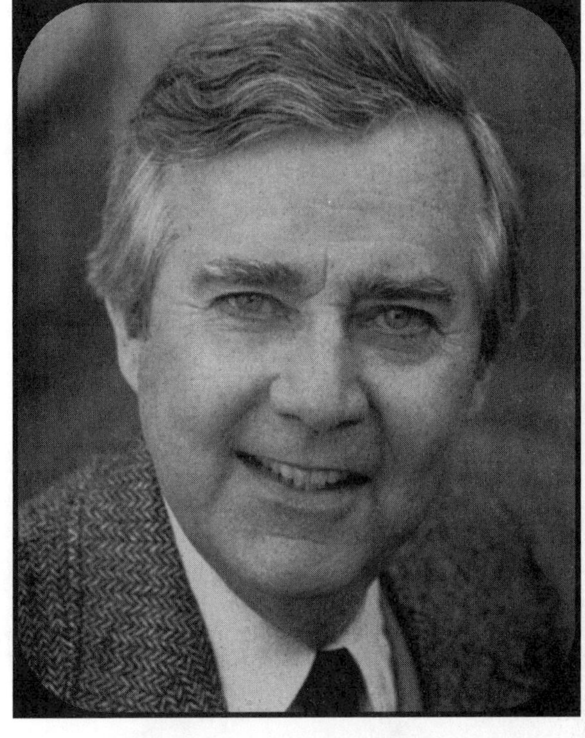

EDDIE DEEZEN

Eddie is very busy these days doing commercials for television. He loves doing voice-overs for radio and animation. He told me about his career since *Grease*.

"I did a lot of movies after *Grease*, of course, but none of them nearly as big. I did *War Games* and *I Want to Hold Your Hand* and also Steven Spielberg's *1941*. I got to work with John Belushi, who was very nice. I do mostly voice-overs now—lots of Taco Bell commercials, and I was the voice of Pop for Rice Krispies for four years."

Eddie lives in Hollywood, California, and has a sweet pet chinchilla named Roscoe. I asked him the question.

"Eugene 20 years later? He would be a nerd—a nerd, a nerd, a nerd. A grown-up nerd, but definitely still a nerd. I guess I see him as a high-tech nerd, working with computers, developing these weird applications that only two or three people in the world might understand or care about. Or maybe he's into some kind of weird science. Yeah, genetic engineering! He spends his days in some top-secret biology lab, crossbreeding weird vegetables, creating new species. He's, like, developing the world's healthiest tomato, the world's juiciest orange, a high-protein nectarine, that kind of thing. He works really long hours in this basement laboratory monitoring his experiments. And he's still really skinny, and he lives on Hostess Twinkies."

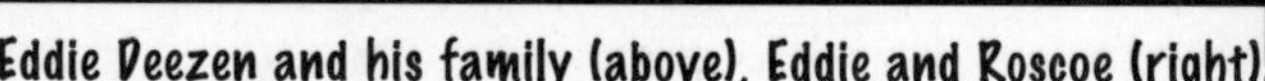

Eddie Deezen and his family (above), Eddie and Roscoe (right).

EDD BYRNES

Edd wrote a terrific new book, *Edd Byrnes, Kookie No More*, published by Barricade Books. He's been traveling all around the country doing book signings. Edd has performed and lived all over the world. He currently resides in Beverly Hills and appreciates the fine art of gourmet cooking, particularly oriental and Italian cuisines.

> *Didi*: So what do you think Vince Fontaine would be doing twenty years later?
> *Edd*: Vince? Oh, he'd be picking up women on Sunset Boulevard, getting in trouble. Oh boy!

DARRELL ZWERLING

Darrell Zwerling was Mr. Lynch in *Grease*. He was the teacher that almost caught Sonny spiking the punch at the dance-off.

His other film credits include: *And Justice for All, The Main Event, High Anxiety, Chinatown, Doc Savage, Lady Liberty,* and many more.

He has been in numerous television movies and guest-starred on "Murder She Wrote," "Dynasty," "House Calls," "Columbo," "Barney Miller," and "Kojak," to name a few.

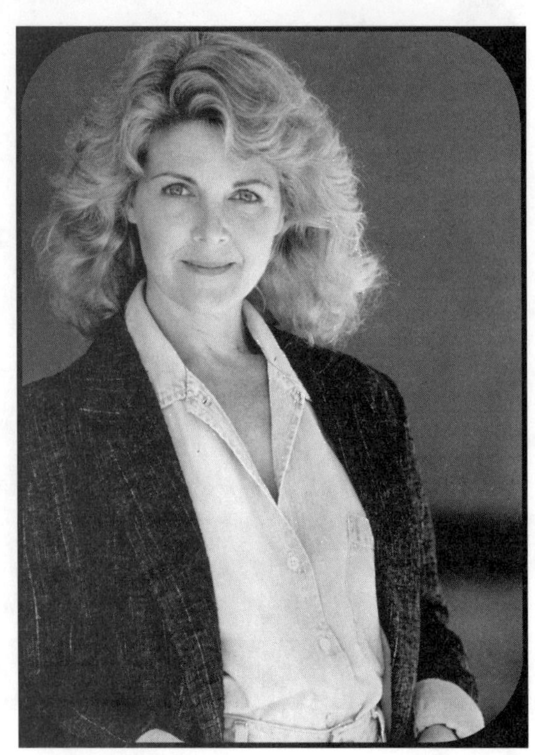

DANCERS

CAROL CULVER

"Since Grease, I was in a few other movie musicals, choreographed a few TV shows and rock videos, and coached a number of celebrities (tap dancing mostly) for movies they had to dance in.

"But then along came a thing called *The Harmonic Convergence* and I got "the call," so to speak. I got very active in the New Age movement and dropped out of show biz. I have coordinated workshops for a number of authors, healers, and teachers. I have been a program director for many large New Age events and produced benefits.

"All that leads to where I am now. I am getting married and moving to Kauai, Hawaii. I plan to teach dance and acting classes there, among other things. I will be editing books and finishing my own book, *For the Time Being: A Magical Medicine Fable*. My fiancé is a very talented graphic designer and Web master. Together we are developing a website that serves to enhance one's well-being."

MIMI LIEBER

"I did a film opposite Dennis Quaid a couple of years ago that nobody saw in which I played the snake lady in the circus. I've guest-starred on just about every show on television, I've done great movies, and I've gone on national tours of Broadway shows."

Left: Mimi guest-starring on "Seinfeld."

SEAN MORAN

I just saw Sean in a terrific role on "N.Y.P.D. Blue." He has been guest starring on lots of television shows, including, "E.R.," "Parenthood" and "Dr. Quinn, Medicine Woman." He just finished shooting a movie for the History Channel entitled *Nero, My Son*, in which he played the title role. Also, Sean has been writing and directing. He recently wrote a kid's movie, *Mud Alley Midgets*, for release during Christmas, 1998. His directorial credits include *Nunsense* and *Jesus Christ Superstar.*

Sean lives in Studio City, California, but is very close to his folks and family in Vermont. "Vermont is my real home, and I love and miss my family very much!"

RICHARD WEISMAN

Since *Grease*, Richard appeared in the films *Grease 2* and *Sgt. Pepper*. He recently played the apostle Thomas in a production of *Jesus Christ Superstar* in Hollywood. Richard is the art director for Merle Norman Cosmetics at their corporate headquarters. He is very proud of a one-man show of his art in Venice, California, that displayed fifty-three of his paintings and photographs.

Richard has traveled to Europe half a dozen times, visiting England, Scotland, France, Spain, Portugal, Italy, Greece and Malta. One highlight of his European travels was seeing Stockard Channing in London in a production of *Six Degrees of Separation*. For fun, Richard went to UCLA extension and took classes in painting, production design for film, French, Italian, and even polo.

JENNIFER BUCHANAN

Jenny has been very busy guest-starring on lots of television shows, including "Home Improvement," "Thunder Alley," "Brand New Life," and "Another World." Her film credits include *The Postman* and *The Bodyguard* for Warner Brothers and *One Day Pass* for the American Film Institute. She has been performing in many different theaters in Los Angeles in a variety of plays.

Jenny participated in a rigorous internship for two years with Marge McClenon, a well-known yogini in the Pasadena area. Jenny loves teaching yoga for many reasons. "I am an experienced practitioner and teacher of hatha yoga. My current resumé includes three years of teaching beginning through intermediate/advanced classes, as well as yoga for people in recovery, or with life-threatening illnesses, and yoga in preparation for religious meditation."

Jenny and her son, Joseph, live in Pasadena, California.

DENNIS DANIELS

Dennis has been acting, singing, and dancing in eight different Broadway musicals in the last few years. I saw him in Hal Prince's production of *Showboat*, and he was superb. He is living in New Jersey and recently has been focusing more on directing, choreographing, and creating new projects. Also, Dennis has been traveling in the U.S. and abroad, teaching, choreographing, and judging world-competitive baton twirlers.

LOU SPADACCINI

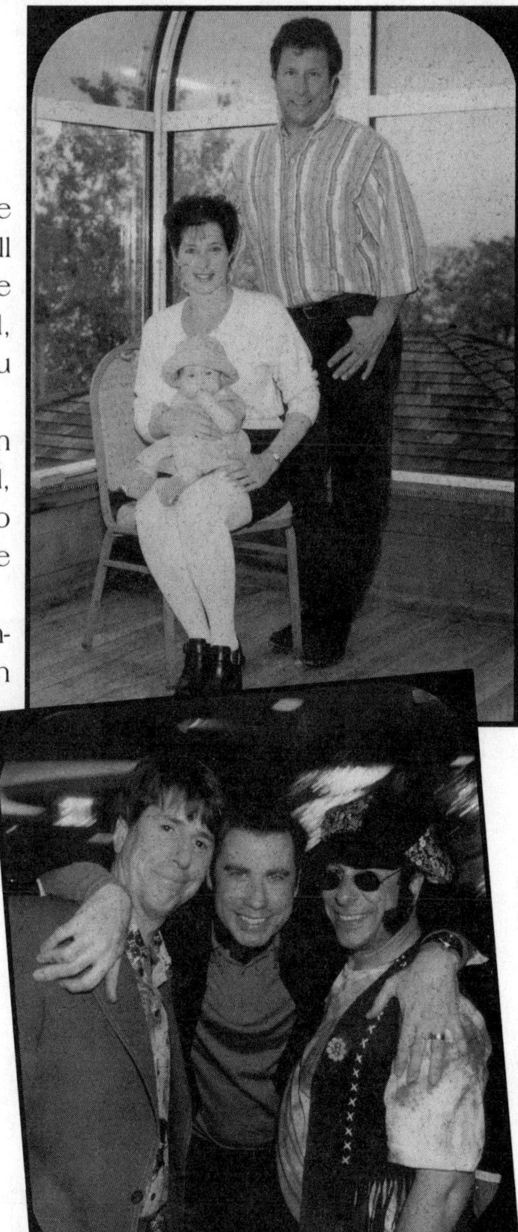

Lou played Woppo. At all the *Grease* parties, he and Andy Tennant were my dance partners. I'll never forget a New Year's Eve party at Olivia's house in Malibu. She put a big dance floor over her pool, and I had the pleasure of dancing with Andy and Lou all night!

Lou got married in 1991 to beautiful Karen, from Suffern, New York. "We met through a mutual friend, and we just got along from day one. Two years ago Karen gave birth to our daughter, Jenna Marie, and we just bought our first home in Mar Vista, California."

Lou is now working on the other side of the camera. "I am a video technician. I do video assists, which is something you might be familiar with. On film cameras they have a little tap inside the film camera, a video camera which generates a video signal. And we provide monitors and tape decks and tape so the director can see right away exactly what is being put down on film. And I've been doing commercials, a lot of commercials (and I've enjoyed it)."

DAN LEVANS

Began his professional career at the age of nine tap dancing with a touring carnival and variety shows. Later became a Principal Dancer with the American Ballet Company, American Ballet Theatre, and New York City Ballet, working with Jerome Robbins, Agnes de Mille, Anthony Tudor, Eliot Feld, Eugene Loring and George Balanchine. He appeared in the New York City Opera production of *Street Scene*, choreographed by Pat Birch. Film and television appearances include *Red Badge of Courage*, *The Silence*, *The Waltons*, *Can't Stop the Music*, and *Turningpoint*.

Dan has choreographed theater productions of *Anything Goes*, *West Side Story*, *Bloomergirl*, *Cabaret*, *Miss*

Liberty, Brimstone, Oh Boy!, and *My Fair Lady*. He has directed and choreographed musical reviews for the St. Regis Hotel in New York City, and his first off-Broadway production, *Amphigorey*, was nominated for a Drama Desk award. A member of Society of Stage Directors & Choreographers, Dan lives and teaches in New York City when not globe-trotting with work.

ANDY TENNANT

When I spoke to Andy he was in the medieval market town of Sarlat in southwest France. He was directing his fourth major motion picture, a realistic version of the *Cinderella* story with Anjelica Huston, Drew Barrymore, and Jeanne Moreau. I knew he had become a successful film director, and I was very curious how it happened:

"I got my first break in 1988 directing "The Wonder Years," and my first feature film was *It Takes Two* with the Olsen twins. I also directed *Fools Rush In* with Matthew Perry. Now, I'm in a beautiful village in the south of France with horses and armor, and I'm having a blast."

Andy got married five years ago to a fashion designer, Sharon Johnson. They were blessed with triplets, and on November 22, 1997, Sharon gave birth to a baby boy named Sawyer.

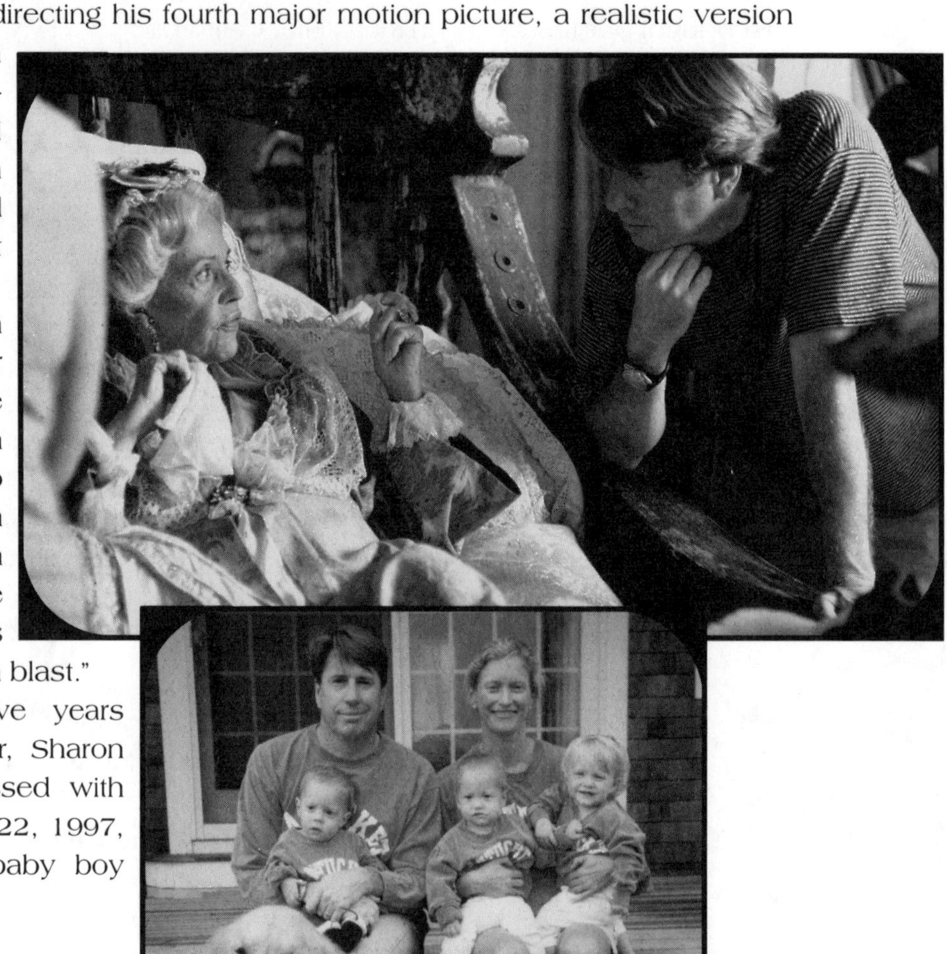

Andy Tennant directing Jeanne Moreau (above), and Andy with his wife Sharon, their triplets McKenna, Sydney, and Judd, and dog Sconset.

CREATIVE STAFF

RANDAL KLEISER

Randal just finished directing Melanie Griffith and Tom Berenger in *Shadow of a Doubt*. When I asked him what he was interested in working on in the future, he told me that he is "now developing three science fiction movies. My brother does incredible special effects, and we are trying to decide which movie to do next."

Randal and cast of feature film *It's My Party* (right), and with *Honey, I Blew Up the Kid*'s Rick Moranis (above).

PAT BIRCH

Pat's sexy and fanciful style worked brilliantly in *First Wives Club*—she choreographed the final number of the film where Goldie Hawn, Diane Keaton, and Bette Midler sing "You Don't Own Me." She is working with Adrian Mitchell and Richard Peaslee on an adaptation of Hans Christian Andersen's *The Snow Queen*. It will be presented at the New York State Theater Institute and then at London's Unicorn Theater, with a New York debut scheduled for 1998. Pat is also collaborating with Bill Hoffman and Melissa Manchester on a new musical called *On a Saturday Night*. She's very enthusiastic about this project, "a brand new millennium piece all about Saturday night." Pat is working on *Band In Berlin*, a multimedia project about singers in Germany in the late 1920s and early 1930s.

Pat and her husband, Bill Becker, are awaiting the birth of their second grandchild.

Louis St. Louis.

LOUIS ST. LOUIS

Louis St. Louis is currently the worldwide musical supervisor for *Smokey Joe's Cafe*, overseeing the long-running Broadway production as well as the national tour and companies in Australia and London. The musical's cast album won the 1996 Grammy Award for Best Musical Show. As a conductor and arranger, he has worked with Chita Rivera, Ann-Margret, Debbie Allen, Lesley Gore, and Lily Tomlin. He was the musical director for the Emmy Award-winning special *Lily/Sold Out* and *Lily for President*. As a composer and lyricist, Louis has two major musicals in the works, *Sugar Hill* and an adaptation of Emily Brontë's *Wuthering Heights*.

JOEL THURM

1998 finds Joel Thurm both producing and casting for film and television in Los Angeles. He is currently producing a feature film for Citadel Production and a miniseries for ABC. Last year he produced the United Artists' feature film *It's My Party*, which was written and directed by Randal Kleiser.

Since 1994 Joel has raised over $125,000.00 for various AIDS organizations by bicycling in the California and New York-Boston AIDS Rides.

Joel Thurm at California AIDS Ride.

MAXINE FOX LORENCE

Maxine and her wonderful husband Larry Lorence have spent the last few years in the beautiful Blue Ridge Mountains countryside outside of Charlottesville, Virginia. Maxine is now the producing director of StageWorks. She is "in the process of creating an unusual theatrical production company. With the mandate of bringing New York-quality theater to central Virginia, StageWorks will create an off-Broadway experience in Charlottesville. What's unusual? This company is a fusion of profit and not-for-profit theater, run with the best instincts of both. So while we'll need financing in the beginning, after a short while we intend to be self-supporting."

Maxine Fox Lorence and Larry Lorence.

KEN WAISSMAN

Ken Waissman is a Tony Award-winning producer whose track record includes the two longest-running dramas of the 1980s: *Agnes of God* and *Torch Song Trilogy*.

In 1992, Ken commissioned J.P. Miller to adapt his screenplay *Days of Wine and Roses* for the stage.The resulting production had its world premiere at the Cleveland Playhouse.

Currently, Ken is producing *Street Corner Symphony*, a Broadway musical retrospective of the pop and soul music of the 1960s and 1970s. It opened on November 18, 1997, at the Brooks Atkinson Theater.

Me and Broadway producer Ken Waissman.

JIM JACOBS

In 1992, Jim received a Humanitarian Award from the Young Adult Institute in New York for "setting an outstanding example of the socially conscious citizen through his involvement in, and commitment to, seeking a better world for those less fortunate than ourselves." Currently, *Grease*, the stage musical, continues to break box office records with long-running, full-scale professional productions in Australia, London, Italy, Holland, Greece, Germany, Austria, Switzerland, the Far East, and on Broadway (again!). Jim has also coauthored several other plays and musicals, including *Island of Lost Coeds*, *Bats in the Belfry*, and *Remember the Night*. He and his talented wife, Denise Nettleton, live in southern California.

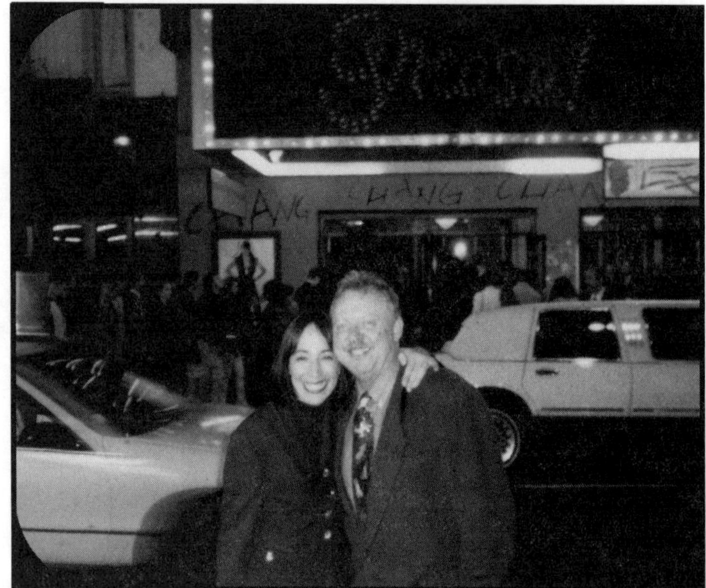

Jim Jacobs and me at Eugene O'Neill Theater.

DIDI CONN

I've been costarring on a PBS series for children, "Shining Time Station," for the last eight years. I took the job largely to meet Ringo Starr, who was playing Mr. Conductor. Ringo was replaced by George Carlin after the first season, and George is a great guy, too. Parents of the kids who watch the show are really impressed that I got to work with a Beatle. Their kids, however, don't think it's such a big deal—they think a beetle is a bug! I have made some great friends working on such a long-running series. Brian O'Connor, who plays Schemer, is one of the most generous and hilarious actors I know.

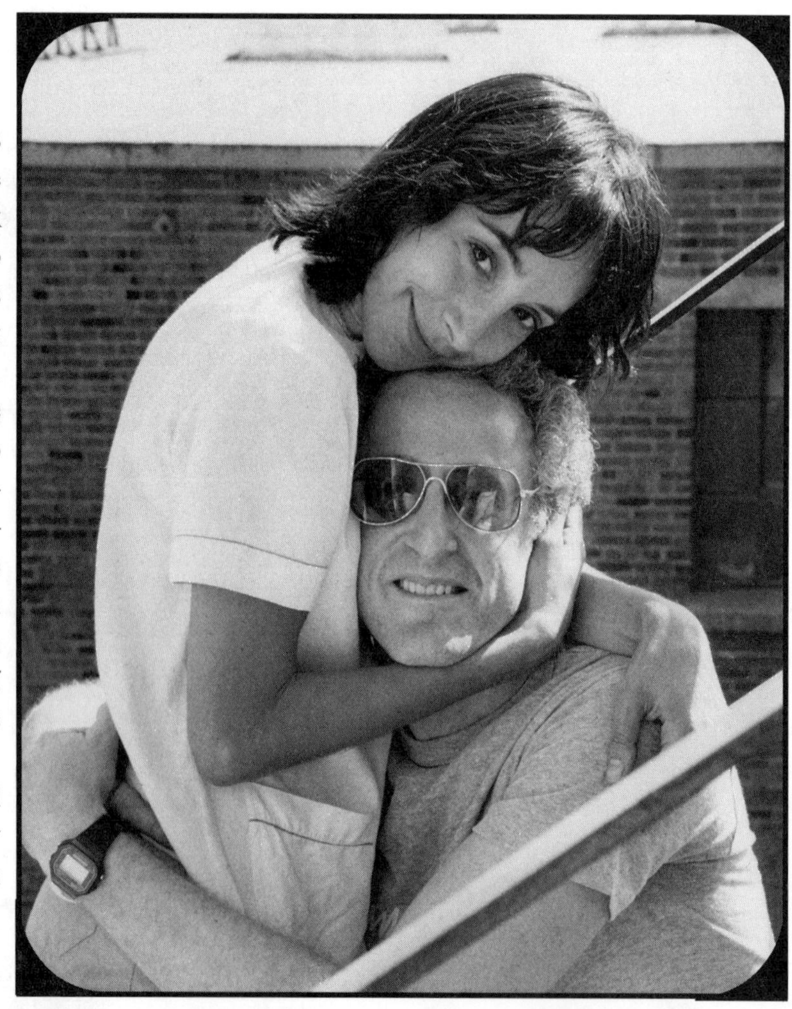

Five years ago, my husband, David Shire, and I adopted a beautiful baby boy. His name is Daniel, and he's an adorable ball of energy. We moved to New York from Los Angeles two and a half years ago and live in a wonderful rural community in the Hudson Valley, about a thirty-minute drive from Manhattan.

When you grow up in Brooklyn and you want to act, all you dream about is being on Broadway one day. Four years ago, I made my Broadway debut in Neil Simon's *Lost in Yonkers*. It was one of the highlights of my career. I played the lead role of Bella, and it was very challenging. The audiences gave us standing ovations every night! Last year, I recorded a CD for children, *Mommy, Gimme a Drinka Water*. It's a song cycle originally

Opposite page: Me and my husband, David Shire. This page: Fascimile of CD cover of *Mommy, Gimme a Drinka Water* (top), me, Barry Pearl, and his wife, Heather, backstage (above, left and right).

recorded by Danny Kaye in the 1950s. I recorded it with a thirty-piece orchestra with orchestrations by Tony and Academy Award-winner Jonathan Tunick. The thirteen songs are all from the point of view of a child's heart and soul, and I had a great time singing them.

I am blessed with a super husband. He is a film, television, and theater composer who has won an Academy Award and several Grammys, and written a number of Broadway and off-Broadway shows. When I was in Los Angeles taping the series "Benson," I was staying with my dear friends Peter Hay and Dorthea Atwater. I had a radio in my room, and one night I was listening to a program hosted by film composer David Raksin, who was interviewing David. He was funny and modest and his music was unusually moving. They were playing themes from *Farewell, My Lovely*, costarring Charlotte

Me, my mom, and my three brothers (upper left), me and my son Daniel (left), Daniel and my stepson, Matt (below), me and my father, Leonard Bernstein (right).

Rampling. David said how much he enjoyed scoring this movie, because he'd always had a crush on her. Right then and there I decided I was going to call him up, pretend I was Charlotte Rampling, and ask him out. I called, and in my deepest sexiest voice said, "Hello, David, this is Charlotte," and then I cracked up. I asked him out and he said yes! He told me later that even if he hadn't been interested in going out with me—which wasn't the case—he would have, because he figured anyone who had the courage to do what I did must have spent a great deal of money on therapy!

David and I just celebrated our fourteenth anniversary! I also have a terrific stepson named Matt, a twenty-two-year-old hunk, who lives in Los Angeles and works in the film industry. We have a sweet and loyal dog, Romeo, a West Highland terrier, who is six years old.

The cast of "Benson" (above), and the cast of "Shining Time Station" (right).

So what is old Frenchy doing twenty years later? I asked myself.

Frenchy is alive and well and living on Ocean Parkway in Brooklyn, where she is the owner and chief operator of her own beauty parlor. She is a single mom who relates well to her 12-year-old son, gives free buzz cuts to his friends, and has a number of old faithful customers who span a cross-section of generations, including elderly blue-haired ladies in the neighborhood, some of them her mother's friends, who come in for their weekly 'do's. But the salon hasn't ever been quite successful enough, and so Frenchy makes her real living as a dog groomer in an adjoining room.

Frenchy today in her dog grooming salon (above), and me today (left).

In Loving Memory

It is with deep sadness that I recall the loss of a number of people who were involved with *Grease*: Bronte Woodard, our screenwriter; Warren Casey, coauthor of the Broadway musical; my sweet and loving friend Gary Kalkin, who was the unit publicist; the beautiful and talented Joan Blondell, who played Vi; Eve Arden, who so wonderfully played our principal, Mrs. McGee; Dennis C. Stewart, who played Leo, the leader of the Scorpions; the warm and talented Tommy Smith, a colleague and close friend of Pat Birch; and the dynamic dancer Greg Rosatti.

All of the people I spoke to in compiling this book were deeply saddened by the passing of these dear friends and valued colleagues. We all wish to send our heartfelt love and condolences to their families.

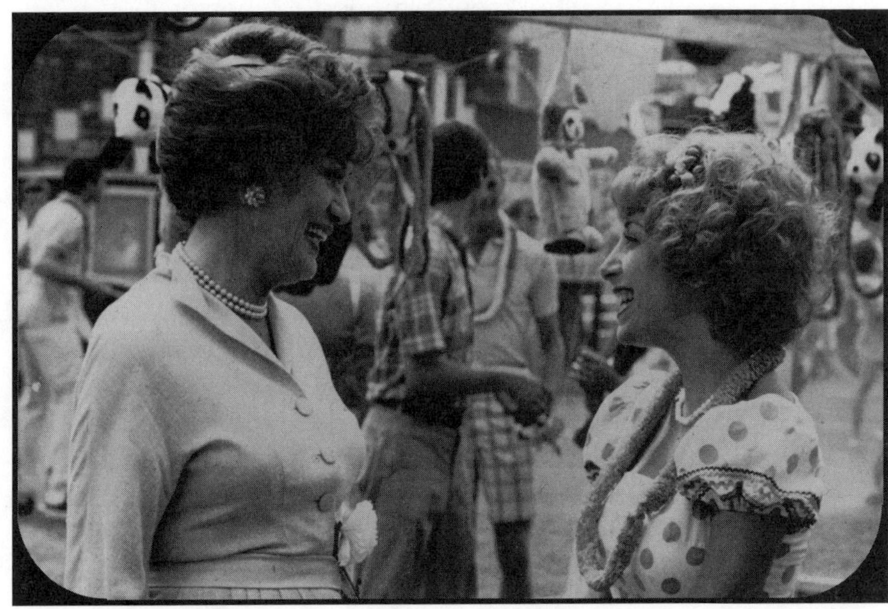

Eve Arden's son, Douglas West, remembers how exciting it was to visit his mother while she was filming *Grease*. "Here it is, twenty years later, and I get to watch that same excitement in the eyes of my eight-year-old daughter, Devon, who has discovered this marvelous film for herself. She absolutely adores *Grease*, not just because her grandmother was in it, but because it means something to her. She has memorized all the songs, figured out all the dance steps, and performs them regularly in front of her mirror. Next season, Devon will also become a member of the extended *Grease* family when she joins the cast of a local production being done by the Children's Theater Network."

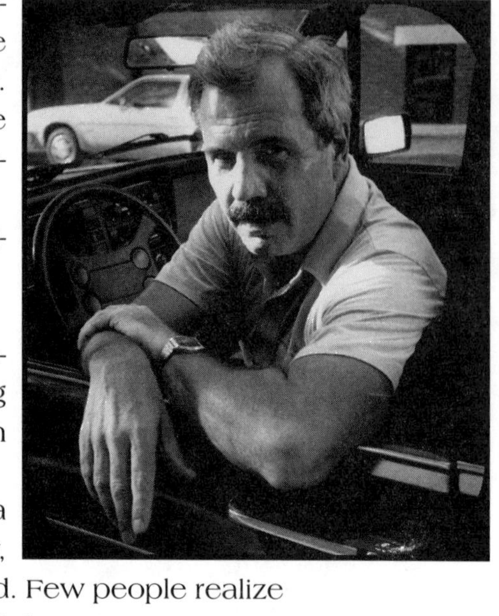

Jim Jacobs sent me this beautiful remembrance of his longtime friend and collaborator, Warren Casey:

> "When Warren Casey and I first met at a small Chicago community theater in the spring of 1963, we were both budding young amateur actors cast in a memorably bad production of *A Shot in the Dark*.
>
> "Although Warren was eight years older than me, and a recently transplanted New Yorker, we hit it off immediately, and within a year he had become my undisputed best friend. Few people realize how long we knew each other (seven years) before our collaboration on *Grease* began.
>
> "During the course of the next twenty-five years our friendship and professional partnership never ceased to continually remind me of one basic truth: This guy was a genius. Math, science, art as well. He was, without question, the funniest man I have ever known in my life. No one has ever made me laugh as much, and as often, as Warren Casey. I'm often reminded by my wife of the time Warren showed up quite unexpectedly in Las Vegas, moments before my second marriage was to take place. (He had been best man at my first wedding thirteen years earlier.) With the scheduled ceremony about to begin, I hastily asked Warren if he'd like to be my best man once again. 'Sure, why not?' he deadpanned. 'It's a tradition.'
>
> "In November 1988, Warren Casey passed away. The loss to those of us who knew him (and to theater fans everywhere) is immeasurable. His humor, his songs, and his lyrics will continue to live on every night somewhere in the world, wherever *Grease* is being performed. You can rest assured that Warren is here in spirit—just the way we always remember him."

Pat Birch sent me these thoughts about Tommy Smith:

"Our quiet smiling Tommy took care of us, laughed with us, sorted out schedules, problems, kept us going when it was rough. Tommy, our gentleman greaser, always there. Still here. I miss you, Tommy."

And Larry Mark sent me a beautiful photo of Gary Kalkin and a very touching letter:

October 2, 1997
Dear Didi,

As you know, *Grease* and Gary and I have a wonderful history. While I ran publicity at Paramount during the making and the release of *Grease*, Gary was the unit publicist during the shoot and special publicist coordinating all publicity activities at the time of release.

Gary was my best and my oldest friend, and the last New Year's Eve we spent together (1994–1995), we had a very quiet, reflective evening—and when we put the television on, there was *Grease*. We naturally watched it to the end—recalling certain moments during the filming and during the subsequent hoopla surrounding the movie. We reminisced about the various people we had gotten to know and about the terrific times that *Grease* had provided. All in all, it inspired us to look over our lives and to get a bit nostalgic.

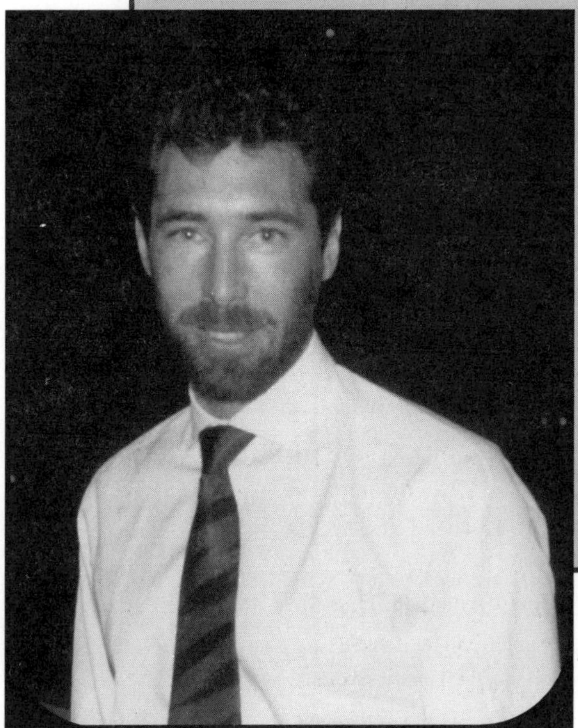

Gary died five days later. Not ever convinced that we were about to be separated, *Grease*, in that last viewing, gave us the opportunity to come together yet again in a meaningful way, and for that I will always be grateful. Though Gary and I are far away from each other right now, I'd like to think that "we'll always be together."

With love,
Larry

CONCLUSION

Confession time! Now I'm going to be perfectly honest with you. Most of us were not, as I've been telling you, just a "tad" or a "little" older or even *more* than a little older than the characters we were playing. Most of us were *much* older. In fact, Joel Thurm told me that they did a crow's-feet test on all of us at our final callback. If we had those telltale lines at the edges of our eyes, we were *too* old! But we got away with it because *Grease* is bigger than life. It isn't reality—it is heightened reality, idealized reality.

The characters we played and, indeed, we actors who played them as well, all wanted to belong to a group and be identified with that group, and we'd do anything to stay in the club. The stakes were high, and the potent energy that blasted out from every pore of every one of the cast members was reciprocated by Randal, Allan, Pat, Louis, Joel, Bill, Jerry, Lynn, Paula, Richard, Joyce, Neil Machlis, Christine my hairdresser, Dan my makeup man, Betty and Bruce, and all the other great, hardworking, talented people who were on the other side of the camera. They were the most loving, kind, and supportive guardians we wild kids could have ever hoped to have.

Michael Tucci, Dan Striepeke, our very talented makeup artist, and Joan Blondell.

We never stopped moving. We rehearsed and shot in fifth gear all day long, but there was always someone catching us to change us into a dry shirt, or caress us softly with a powder puff or a comb, or give us a cold drink or a spritz of Sea Breeze—anything. Our wonderful support team applauded our takes and treated us like princes and princesses, and we blossomed and were recharged by all that pampering. It wasn't about money or ego gratification. It was just plain exciting for us to be in a major motion picture. We had top veterans in the film industry to guide us and serve as role models. They set the high standards that we emulated. Maybe that's one big reason why *Grease* is so popular, and it all stems from the love and respect that kept bouncing back and forth in the universe we all created for the purpose of sheer entertainment.

It was a joy of joys to reconnect with all my old friends for this book. Most of us have gone on to jobs and lives that have taken us to emotional and physical places we never could have imagined for ourselves.

I once had a teacher tell me not to get hung up on my numerical age because, she was convinced, each of us is all ages at all times. I think she's right. Maybe I'll go now and call Frankie Avalon. It would be so dreamy to be seventeen again and hear him singing, "Turn in your teasing comb and go back to high school."

Why not? I got a direct line to that "malt shop in the sky."

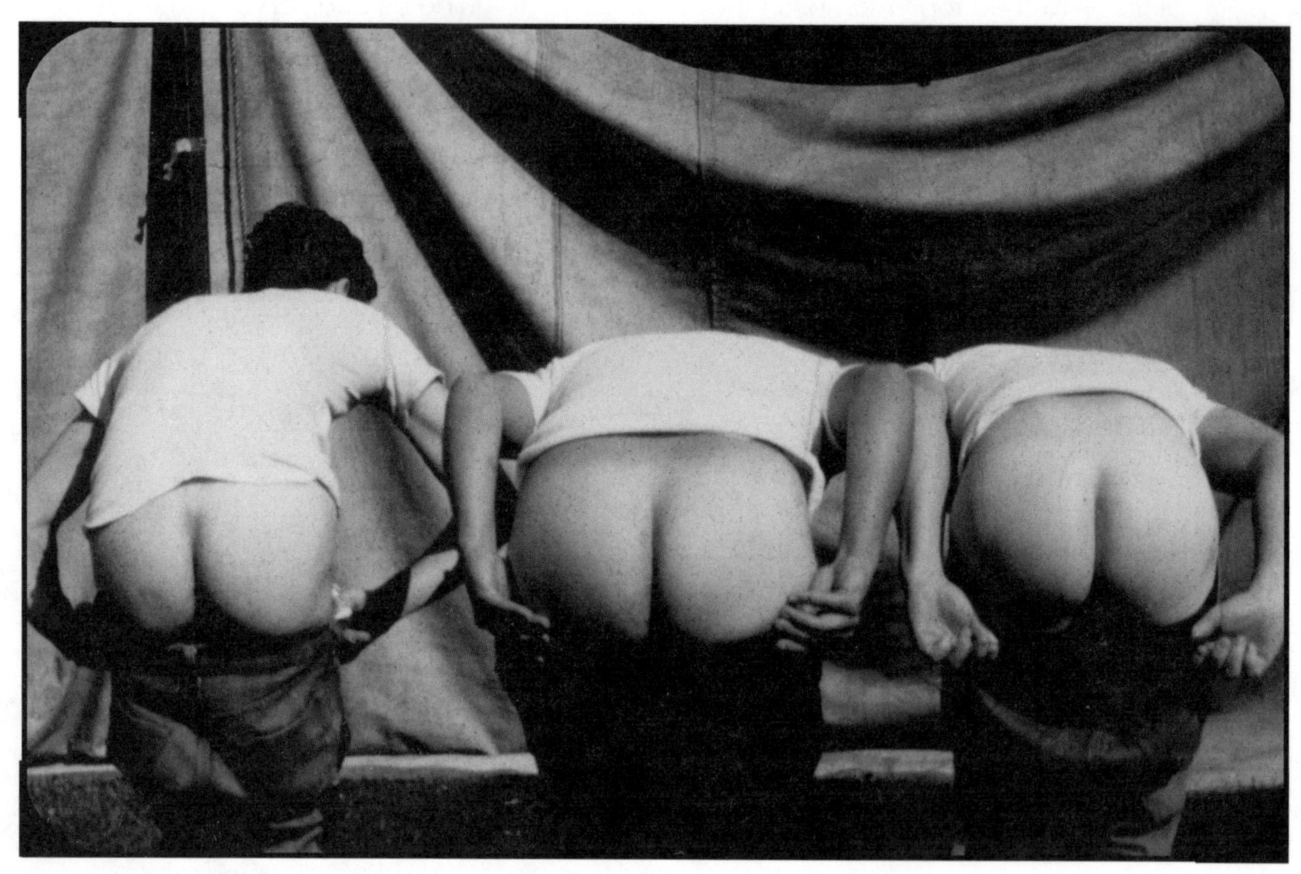

The End

ACKNOWLEDGMENTS

Yes, I've often gotten by with a little help from my friends. But this book would not exist without a *lot* of help from many of them. I have never felt so loved and supported in my life. Everyone I called could not have been more helpful. First and foremost, of course, I want to thank all of my amazing and talented *Grease*-mates, who have been so generous with their time and memories. They gave me hours and hours of interviews and entrusted me with their precious photographs, many of them taken right out of frames on their walls to be sent to me. Without their memories—and *my* memories of their indelible work—this book would not exist. (I promise, guys, I'll get all the photographs back to you—I promise!)

This project began when I came upon a big box in my mother Beverly Shmerling's basement that was filled with candid photographs she had taken and memorabilia she had saved. I told my influential and supportive buddy Freddie Gershon my idea and he told me to take it to Allan Carr.

I can never thank Allan Carr enough for all his encouragement and support. His confidence and enthusiasm in my writing motivated and inspired me, and he generously volunteered to write his facinating foreword to this book. Also, Allan introduced me to Alan Nevins, who believed in the project enough to become my first literary agent.

The project never would have happened without the support of my two dear friends, John Travolta and Olivia Newton-John, who have been behind me a hundred and ten percent all the way.

If all lawyers were like Susan Schaefer, there would be no lawyer jokes. My gratitude to her for clearing the way through the legal jungles that threatened at many a juncture to bring this project to a halt.

Lisa Jenner Hudson, my editor from Hyperion, is a genuine *Grease*-ophile. Her enthusiasm and sense of humor made this project a joy for me. And I'm grateful to Risa Kessler at Paramount for remembering how much Lisa wanted to do a book about *Grease*. Thanks to her, also, for digging into the Paramount archives for Dave Friedman's superb photographs.

Randal Kleiser, our gorgeous, fearless leader, dug up some classic candid shots. His friendship and contributions have been invaluable. Special thanks to his terrific assistant, Kenneth Brady.

Dear friend Larry Mark sent me a treasure trove of publicity material, which was extremely useful to me.

Jane Estrin has been an amanuensis extraordinaire—a Girl Friday and all the other days of the week as well. Her organizational, typing, and dictation skills, computer wisdom, friendship, and creative ideas made her an indispensable resource. And she can cook, too! My gratitude also to her husband, Mitchell, and son William for giving her up for the major part of the two months that we worked together. I love you, guys.

My Yale-grad husband, an English as well as music major, cleaned up my grammar, punctuation, and syntax, entertained Daniel, held my hand (and the rest of me) into the wee hours, and was another invaluable sounding board. He is my professional, hard-working, deadline-meeting role model and my best friend.

My little boy, Daniel, was enormously patient with me when I had to push him away from our computer and have his father put him to bed. (How Daniel made me laugh when he watched *Grease* for the first time and remarked, "Mommy has red hair just like Madeline!") I'm also grateful to his warm and loving teacher, Julie Wood.

Tom Schmall kept an additional computer humming, making tape transcriptions, and worked along with Jane Estrin on many a potentially overwhelming day.

My brilliant cousin, Ellen Bernstein, gave me some significant help with the "This Is Now" chapter. At a particularly challenging time in her life, she managed to find a great deal of time to help me enormously.

My dear friend and teacher, Catherine Shainberg, kept my soul intact and my will focused with her enormous faith in my abilities.

Very special thanks to Robert Miller, Carol Smith, David Cashion, Claudyne Bedell, Christine Weathersbee, David Lott, Audra Zaccaro, Victor Weaver, David Cohen, and John Marius at Hyperion for their supportive and colorful contribution.

The love and support of so many other friends and relatives helped make this book happen, and I would be remiss if I did not list them all: Leonard and Patricia Bernstein, Bradley and Suk Wah Bernstein, Andrew D. Bernstein and Stephanie Bardey, Richard Bernstein, Matt Shire, Rachel Lehmann, Sandy Shmerling and family, Sandy Shire, Hilary Laddin, Marj Blauman, Tina and Albert Boardman, Julie and Charlotte Bernstein, Hildy Bernstein, Noah Graham, Gerry, Susan, and Sarah Bernstein, Lisa Gottlieb, Annette Anglisano, Paul Lieber and Gwenn Victor, Serafina Restaino, Maria Lopez, Doris Allen, Lois Mendelson, Anita Miller, Freda Attinson, Diane Augelletta, Alyssa Cohen, Laurie Meinberg, Gineen Weiss,Victoria Fairbanks, Debra Girshner, Jo Baer, David Shaul, Mark Redanty, Betty Fanning, Marty Litke, Ethan Phillips, Nina Nisenholtz, Aviva Gross, Vivianne Lind, Jeff Geibelson, Dawn Nepp, Brian O'Connor, Irene Worth, Janice Kent, Jim Caswell and Sidsie Davis, Britt Allcroft, Nancy Chapelle, Rick Siggelkow, Millissa Arena, Cindy Bernstein, Bob Gersh, Frank Conn, Richard and Janet Maltby, John and Lila Weidman, William and Georgie Cutter, the Jeffrey and Lynne Sandhaus family, Roy Gerber, Ron Taft, Steven Rowley, Denise Nettleton. Chloe Lattanzi, Pat Farrar, Bill Butler, John Burnett, Howard Murad, Norman Stiles, Abby Tetenbaum, Michael Zager, Milton Schafer, Ellen Schmall, Arnold Aleskovsky, Larry Beiman, my first acting teacher, Harris Sarney, the Roth family, and last but not least, my trusty and indispensible FedEx man, Frank Ietto.

AUTHOR'S NOTE

A scholarship fund is being established with a portion of the royalties from this book for the Therapeutic Nursery at the J.C.C. on the Palisades in Tenafly, New Jersey.

Me with the staff of the Therapeutic Nursery at the J.C.C. on the Palisades. (Back row: Me, Lois Mendelson, Anita Miller. Front row: Laurie Meinberg, Freda Attinson, Alyssa Cohen, Doris Allen.)

Photo Credits

The credits listed below as © Paramount Pictures *or* © Dave Friedman Photo for Paramount Pictures *represent official movie photography (© 1998 Paramount Pictures and © Dave Friedman Photo for Paramount Pictures. All rights reserved).*

Every effort has been made to identify the photographer or source of each illustration, but in case of any errors, the publisher shall use best efforts to ensure that proper credit will appear when appropriate in all its future editions of this book.

Page vi: (clockwise from upper left) Mimi Lieber; Mimi Lieber; © Paramount Pictures; Beverly Schmerling; © Dave Friedman Photo for Paramount Pictures; Dennis Daniels; (center) Beverly Schmerling

Page 1: © Paramount Pictures

Page 2: Barry Pearl

Page 3: © Dave Friedman Photo for Paramount Pictures

Page 4: Mimi Lieber

Page 5: (top) Allan Carr; (bottom) Andrew D. Bernstein

Page 6: © Paramount Pictures

Pages 7, 8: Didi Conn

Page 9: (top) © Paramount Pictures; (bottom) Jonathan Becker

Page 11: (top) Denise Nettleton; (bottom) Donna Dunlap

Page 13: Tom Moore

Page 14: (top) Pat Birch; (bottom) Tom Moore

Page 15: Carol Culver

Page 16: Barry Pearl

Page 17: Justin Caine

Page 18: Leonard Bernstein

Page 19: Bud Tyne

Page 21: © Paramount Pictures

Page 22: John Travolta

Page 23: (top) John Travolta; (bottom) © Paramount Pictures

Page 24: © Paramount Pictures

Page 25: Olivia Newton-John

Page 26: (top) © Paramount Pictures; (bottom) Randal Kleiser

Page 27: © Paramount Pictures

Page 28: Jeff Conaway

Page 29: (top) Jeff Conaway; (bottom) © Dave Friedman Photo for Paramount Pictures

Pages 30-32: © Paramount Pictures

Page 33: Kelly Ward

Page 34: (top) Susan Buckner; (bottom) © Paramount Pictures

Page 35: © Paramount Pictures

Page 36: Susan Buckner

Page 37: (left) Lorenzo Lamas; (right) © Paramount Pictures

Page 38: (top) Dennis Daniels; (bottom) © Paramount Pictures

Page 39: © Paramount Pictures

Page 40: (top) © Paramount Pictures; (bottom) Rick Perry

Page 41: Mimi Lieber

Page 42: © Dave Friedman Photo for Paramount Pictures

Page 43: © Paramount Pictures

Page 44: (top) Dennis Daniels; (bottom) Susan Buckner

Page 45: (left) Mimi Lieber; (right) Sean Moran

Page 46: Carol Culver

Page 47: (top left, bottom center) Carol Culver; (top right) Antonia Franceschi; (center) Andy Tennant; (bottom left) Sean Moran; (bottom right) Barbi Alison

Page 48: (clockwise from upper left) Carol Culver; Carol Culver; Dennis Daniels; Carol Culver; Dennis Daniels; (center) Pat Birch

Page 49: Barry Pearl

Page 50: Dennis Daniels

Page 51: © Paramount Pictures

Page 52: Beverly Shmerling

Page 53: © Paramount Pictures

Page 54: © Dave Friedman Photo for Paramount Pictures

Page 55: © Dave Friedman Photo for Paramount Pictures

Page 56: (top) Dennis Daniels; (center, bottom) © Paramount Pictures

Page 57: Dennis Daniels

Page 58: © Paramount Pictures

Page 59: Didi Conn

Page 60: (right) © Paramount Pictures; (left) © Dave Friedman Photo for Paramount Pictures

Page 61: © Dave Friedman Photo for Paramount Pictures

Pages 62-66: © Paramount Pictures

Page 67: (left top & bottom) Dennis Daniels; (left center) Barry Pearl; (right) © Paramount Pictures

Page 68: (top) Dennis Daniels; (bottom) Reprinted with the permission of The Topps Company, Inc. © 1978, The Topps Company, Inc.

Pages 69-70: © Paramount Pictures

Page 71: (top) Dennis Daniels; (bottom) © Paramount Pictures

Page 72: © Paramount Pictures

Page 73: (top) © Paramount Pictures; (bottom) © Dave Friedman Photo for Paramount Pictures

Page 75: Dennis Daniels

Page 76: Jeff Conaway

Page 77: (top) © Dave Friedman Photo for Paramount Pictures; (bottom) Mimi Lieber

Pages 79-81: Mimi Lieber

Page 82: Mimi Lieber

Page 83: © Paramount Pictures

Page 84: © Dave Friedman Photo for Paramount Pictures

Page 85: (top left) © Paramount Pictures; (top right) Didi Conn; (bottom) © Dave Friedman Photo for Paramount Pictures

Page 86: © Paramount Pictures

Pages 87-88: © Dave Friedman Photo for Paramount Pictures

Page 89: (top, center) Mimi Lieber; (bottom) © Dave Friedman Photo for Paramount Pictures

Pages 90-91: © Paramount Pictures

Page 92: © Dave Friedman Photo for Paramount Pictures

Page 93: © Paramount Pictures

Page 94: (top) © Dave Friedman Photo for Paramount Pictures; (bottom) Dennis Daniels

Page 95: © Paramount Pictures

Page 96: © Paramount Pictures

Page 97: (top) © Paramount Pictures; (bottom) Lou Spandaccini

Page 98: Susan Buckner

Page 99: (top) Barry Pearl; (bottom) © Dave Friedman Photo for Paramount Pictures

Page 100: Barry Pearl

Page 101: (top) © Dave Friedman Photo for Paramount Pictures; (bottom) Barry Pearl

Page 102: (top) © Dave Friedman Photo for Paramount Pictures; (bottom) Barry Pearl

Page 103: © Paramount Pictures

Page 104: (top) Barry Pearl; (bottom) © Dave Friedman Photo for Paramount Pictures

Page 105: (left, top right) © Paramount Pictures; (bottom right) Randal Kleiser

Page 106: (left) Dennis Daniels; (top right) Pat Birch; (bottom right) Barry Pearl

Page 107: Susan Buckner

Page 108: Barry Pearl

Pages 109-110: © Dave Friedman Photo for Paramount Pictures

Page 111: (top & bottom left) © Dave Friedman Photo for Paramount Pictures; (bottom right) Dennis Daniels

Page 112: © Paramount Pictures

Page 117: (top left) Randal Kleiser; (bottom left, center right, bottom right) Andrew D. Bernstein; (top right) Jim Caswell

Page 118: Andrew D. Bernstein

Page 119: (top right, bottom left) Didi Conn; (top left) Beverly Shmerling; (bottom right) © Paramount Pictures

Page 120: Beverly Shmerling

Page 121: © *GQ: Gentlemen's Quarterly*, courtesy of Conde Nast Publications

Page 122: Bradley Bernstein

Page 123: © Paramount Pictures

Page 124: Barry Pearl

Page 127: John Farrar

Page 128: Olivia Newton-John

Page 129: Penney Clements

Page 131: © Sante D'Orazio

Page 132: © Carol Rosegg

Page 135: (left) Stockard Channing; (top right) © Joan Marcus; (bottom right) © Brigitte LaCombe

Page 136: © Stephen Forman

Page 137: Barry Pearl

Page 138: Kelly Ward

Page 139: Kelly Ward

Page 141: (top) Christopher Barr; (bottom) Dinah Manoff

Page 143: Michael Tucci

Page 144: (top right) © Lisa Hergo; (left) Barry Pearl as Professor Tinkerputt™ in Barney's™ Imagination Island™, © 1994 The Lyons Group. All rights reserved. Used with permission; (bottom) Barry Pearl

Page 147: © Christopher Barr for *Beverly Hills, 213*

Page 149: © Harry Langdon Photography

Page 151: (left, bottom) © Diana Rosen Photography; (right) © Harry Langdon Photography

Page 152: (left) © Stephen Wayda; (right) © Stu Segall

Page 153: (top right) Blanche Mackey; (center left) Dody Goodman; (bottom) © Carol Rosegg

Page 154: (left) Courtesy of CBS Photo Archive; (right) Alice Ghostley; (bottom) Barry Pearl

Page 155: (left) Craig Schwartz; (top right) Pat Lynn; (bottom right) Dick Patterson

Page 156: (top) Cheryl Noday; (bottom left & right) Eddie Deezen

Page 157: (top) Edd Byrnes; (bottom) Darrell Zwerling

Page 158: (top) Attila Aszodi; (bottom) Mimi Lieber

Page 159: (top) Michael Papo; (bottom) Richard Weisman

Page 160: (top) Jennifer Buchanan; (bottom) David Morgan

Page 161: (top, center) Lou Spadaccini; (bottom) Ed Cabana

Page 162: (top) Stephen Morley; (bottom) Andy Tennant

Page 163: (top) Randal Kleiser; (bottom) Pat Birch

Page 164: (top) © Paramount Pictures; (bottom) Dorothy Goulah

Page 165: (top) Maxine Fox Lorence; (bottom) Beverly Shmerling

Page 166: (top) Lisa Hudson; (bottom) Andrew Bernstein

Page 167: (top) © Harry Langdon; (bottom left and right) Jane Estrin

Page 168: (top, bottom center) David Shire; (bottom left) © Elaine Siegel; (bottom right) Didi Conn

Page 169: (left) ABC, Inc.; (right) © Britt Allcroft Inc. 1998

Page 170: (left) © Harry Langdon; (right) Jane Estrin

Page 171: © Paramount Pictures

Page 172: (top) Donna Dunlap; (center, bottom right) Dennis Daniels; (bottom left) © Paramount Pictures

Page 173: Larry Mark

Page 174: Michael Tucci

Page 175: © Paramount Pictures

Page 176: Barry Pearl

Page 179: Beatrice Herrera

Color Photos

Pages 1-2: © Paramount Pictures

Page 3: (clockwise from top right) Carol Culver; Didi Conn; Barry Pearl; © Paramount Pictures; Didi Conn

Page 4: (clockwise from top left) Carol Culver; Susan Buckner; Barry Pearl; Didi Conn; Susan Buckner

Page 5: (top four photos) © Paramount Pictures; (bottom two photos) Barry Pearl

Page 6: (top right, bottom) Barry Pearl; (top left, center right) © Paramount Pictures

Page 7: (top left & right) © Paramount Pictures; (top center & center) Barry Pearl; (bottom) Susan Buckner

Page 8: © Paramount Pictures